BUILDING
FOR A NEW CULTURE II

ARCHITECTURE
CHINA

CONTENTS

Essays

New Trends in Contemporary
Architecture: China and Brazil
Yu Yunlong
Li Xiangning
                                        4

Modernity Redux:
An Introduction to
Contemporary Brazilian
Architecture
Carlos Eduardo Comas
                                        10

A Verandah Conversation
David Leatherbarrow
                                        20

A Map, a Conversation,
and a Bridge
Louise Noelle Gras
                                        38

Figurative Structures:
The Construction of Meaning
in Brazilian Modern
Architecture
Renato Anelli
                                        56

The Culture-driven Urban
Regeneration in Shanghai
Jiang Jiawei
                                        72

Projects

Xitang Market Gallery   78
/ Scenic Architecture Office

Tag Art Museum   90
/ Ateliers Jean Nouvel

Jingdezhen Imperial Kiln Museum   102
/ Studio Zhu Pei

Qintai Art Museum 114
/ Atelier Deshaus

The Cloudscape of Haikou 128
/ MAD Architects

Chapel of Sound 142
/ OPEN Architecture

Laurent Troost 156
Architectures

Metro Arquitetos + 158
Paulo Medes da Rocha

Metro Arquitetos 159

MMBB Arquitetos + 160
Ben-Avid + JPG.ARQ

Paulo Mendes da Rocha + 161
MMBB Arquitetos

SPBR / 162
Baserga Mozzetti
Architett

SPBR / 163
ANGELO BUCCI

Andrade Morettin 164
Architects

Brasil Arquitetura 166

New Trends in Contemporary Architecture: China and Brazil

Yu Yunlong
Post-Doctor, College of Architecture and Urban Planning, Tongji University
Li Xiangning
(Corresponding Author), Dean and Professor, College of Architecture and Urban Planning, Tongji University

Abstract

Based on an international perspective, the examination of contemporary Chinese architecture practices is undergoing a transformation, shifting away from historical reflections toward direct exchanges and away from a reductive dichotomy of East versus West to a more inclusive, multipolar view. Architectural dialogues between distant regions such as China and Brazil have the potential to offer more accurate and diverse insights into the global developments in this field. Based on a review of the lectures, case studies, seminars, and summarizing articles presented at the China–Brazil Architecture Forum on "Modernity as an Ongoing Project," this paper identifies five common themes semi-autonomy, aesthetics of nature, materiality, urbanity, and identity. Through an analysis of these themes and their possible relationship with the two nations of China and Brazil specifically, and global architectural movements in general, the paper explores the insights that the case of Brazil can offer to Chinese scholars researching global contemporary architecture and the international history of architecture.

Keywords
Contemporary Chinese architecture; modernity; architectural discourse

Since the 1990s, the discussion of "contemporary Chinese architecture" has gradually moved toward a global perspective. While in the past it was debated mostly in geographic terms and as a monolithic entity, recent studies have also taken into account its culture and plurality.[1] The architectural dialogue between China and the rest of the globe has also shifted from a dichotomy of East versus West to a standpoint that considers the practical needs of a system that includes multiple cultures and institutional frameworks.[2] Separated by seas and oceans, China and Brazil would appear to be completely isolated from one another. However, since the eighteenth century until the 1970s, the rise and fall of global architectural movements has led to a series of architectural exchanges between the two nations.[3] The great differences in geography and culture between the two countries have led to their independent states of development. Yet, both China and Brazil were deeply influenced by modernity and share similarities in terms of their architectural history,[4] the size of their territories, their geographical diversity, as well as their political and economic development. So what can Chinese architecture contribute to the dialogue with Brazil? The China–Brazil Architecture Forum explored the architectural development trends shared by the two nations. Through an analysis of speeches and research summaries presented at the forum, this paper identifies five common topics of discussion at the forefront of the two nations' architectural development—semi-autonomy, aesthetics of nature, materiality, urbanity and identity—that may act as a framework for subsequent architectural research. These topics can be viewed as a type of dialogue between the two nations' architectural frontrunners, as well as the potential common ground between Chinese architects and the international architectural community.

Quasi-autonomy: Between Tradition and Innovation, Globality and Locality

As one of the keywords for this forum, "ongoing" evokes the dialectic, dynamic relationship between tradition and invention; between locality and globality; and between academic disciplines within and outside the field of architecture.

In his presentation "Re-Imagine: House, School, Bridge," architect Yung Ho Chang elucidated his experiments and creative processes in relation to three specific projects—the Vertical Glass House in Shanghai, the Liangzhu Campus of the China Academy of Art, and the Jishou Art Museum—to arrive at the conclusion that architects in emerging economies have the ability to re-imagine tradition and create revolution. Swiss architect Angelo Pozzoli described his residential project Villa Lugano to offer a new perspective on globality versus locality. Taking inspiration from traditional Brazilian design concepts while adhering to both Switzerland's rigid architectural norms and principles of sustainable development, Pozzoli produced an innovative architectural vision that, though vividly embodying the quintessential characteristics of Brazilian architecture, would be difficult to implement on Brazilian soil. Based on this experience, he concluded that the common belief that globalization leads to homogeneity is not completely accurate. Globalization can actually work with regional traditions to oppose homogeneity.

From a global perspective, architectural historians David Leatherbarrow and Pei Zhao analyzed the ties between China and Brazil in terms of their early exploration of modern architecture. In a speech entitled "A Verandah Conversation," Leatherbarrow analyzed Beaux-Arts architecture and modern architecture's global spread and evolution by reviewing the specific context of Philadelphia in the 1930s, as well as the ties between Paul Philippe Cret, an architect belonging to the Philadelphian School, and Chinese and Brazilian pioneers of modernist architecture, such as Yang Tingbao and Lucio Costa. In "The Early Explorations toward Modernities of Brazilian and Chinese Architecture," Pei examined historical records of exchanges between Liang Sicheng and Oscar Niemeyer in the 1960s and, through a comparison of Liang Sicheng and Lucio Costa's works, shed light on the early development of modernist architecture in Brazil and China.

In "Building a New Tradition," Li Xiangning analyzed how contemporary Chinese architecture explores traditions in order to create new ones that are compatible with the daily lives of citizens today. In "Modernity Redux: An Introduction to Contemporary Brazilian Architecture," Brazilian architectural historian Carlos Eduardo Comas identified three key modernist periods in the history of Brazilian architecture: 1936–1945, 1956–1965 and 1976–1985. Meanwhile, in "The Construction of Meaning in Brazilian Modern Architecture," Brazilian art historian Renato Anelli focused on three main aspects—cultural identity, rapid urbanization, and the social construction of concrete—to explain how, from colonial times to the present day, Brazilian architecture has explored modernity while preserving its traditions, thus creating the imagery of Brazil's "ongoing modernity."

Aesthetics of Nature: Between Pictures of Nature and Natural Landscapes

The relationship between artificial and natural environments has long played an important role in the cultural, aesthetic, and even philosophical traditions of our two nations, and continues to exist at the heart of architectural practices and reflections today.

Wang Shu and Lu Wenyu looked back on their design for the Lin'an History Museum to explain how, in their work, they put a contemporary architectural twist on traditional Chinese landscape paintings. Furthermore, based on the study of local history and geography, landscape paintings, as well as regional annals, Wang and Lu analyzed the specific architectural adaptations to local conditions in the context of residential buildings in the Jiangnan region. While working on the Lin'an History Museum, they transformed their understanding of traditional Chinese landscape paintings into a design strategy that reimagined the relationship between natural elements and built structures.

In "Ecological, Green & Sustainable: Ecological Restoration for a Better Future," member of the Chinese Academy of Engineering Cui Kai explained how, when tasked with designing the Nanjing Horticultural Expo 2021, his reflections on the "scars" left on the natural topography by the former concrete factory on the exhibition ground led him to adopt an architectural strategy of "renovation." By incorporating a variety of existing natural landscapes, he was able to create a green landmark that is both beautiful to behold and provides enjoyable experiences. In doing so, he reincorporated these industrial relics of the city's modernization into its residents' daily lives. Meanwhile, Laurent Troost, an architect hailing from Belgium who has long been based in the Amazon, adopted a design strategy of "architecturizing nature" that combines ecology with economic benefits. For instance, in an abandoned and partly overgrown brick building in the city center of Manaus, he installed lightweight, transparent steel components around the existing vegetation, calling upon the forces of time and nature to diversify the space while respecting its historical value. Through this organic design process, he was able to turn the structure into a new cultural landmark for the city. These projects all reflect the ecological and environmental realities shared between the two developing nations of China and Brazil. Although the case studies differ in terms of approaches and scale, they all use natural means to convert industrial relics into cultural landmarks that are close to the local people.

Through an analysis of his project, the Jingdezhen Imperial Kiln Museum, Zhu Pei argued that the relationship between nature and built structures is the central consideration of architectural design. Using the arched shape of the kilns as a template, he elaborated to create a design for a contemporary space rich in traditional symbolism, which comprises a range of indoor and outdoor spaces and makes use of natural building materials such as bamboo and bricks. Meanwhile, in his project for a weekend residence in São Paulo, Angelo Bucci took advantage of the diversity of tropical flora in the area to craft striking scenery that juxtaposes the building's modern suspended structure with the surrounding vegetation.

Founder of the Metro Arquitetos Associados studio Martin Corullon collaborated with the winner of the Pritzker Architecture Prize, Paulo Mendes da Rocha, to create an "artistic port" in São Paulo, the Cais das Artes. In his speech, Corullon described the aesthetic tension between this work's geometric design and its natural waterside setting, as well as the influence that Paulo Mendes da Rocha and the Paulista School have had on his design process. Although these two architects adopted different design strategies, their works are both experiments in terms of the aesthetic relationship between built architecture and nature.

Materiality: Between Weight and Diversity

The architects from both countries pay attention to the cultural, social, and even philosophical implications of certain building materials and construction techniques. In "Architecture of Craftsmen: Brick & Stone," Zhang Lei presented his process of experimental exploration of using bricks, stone, concrete, and 3D-printed materials in different environments, such as urban or rural areas. He emphasized the way that technical innovations pertaining to the use of certain materials or construction techniques can reshape a building's character and its surroundings, while also offering his reflections on the value of materials for architecture itself.

Meanwhile, architect Vinicius Andrade explained how he designed a multistory cultural building for the IMS Fund using steel frames and glass. Given the building's location on Avenida Paulista, a commercial street in São Paulo's prosperous city center, its construction had to adhere to stringent conditions. He believes that the choice of materials for this project was not purely a response to the limitations imposed by the building site, but also to the changing social perception of materials. Andrade believes that the brutalist concrete aesthetic marked by coarseness and

thickness that was popular throughout Brazil in the second half of the twentieth century is gradually fading, with lightweight and transparent materials such as steel and glass on the rise. The ground floor of the IMS Paulista was lifted above street level to the center of the building and rendered accessible by escalator so that visitors may look down on the street through the floor-to-ceiling glass panes. The engineer for this building was José Luiz Canal who also collaborated with Portuguese architect Álvaro Siza on the Museum for the Iberê Camargo Foundation in Porto Alegre. Canal expressed that the choice of building materials is not merely a technical issue. Engineers and architects must also consider materials' texture and social implications.

Urbanity: Between Public Spaces and Social Action

In his presentation "Regeneration of Industrial Sites along Huangpu River," architect Liu Yichun explained how the series of works he created along the bank of the Huangpu River in Shanghai contributed to this industrial canal's transformation into an urban space. While respecting its fundamental structure, Liu successfully converted an abandoned industrial building into the Long Museum, an artistic space. Meanwhile, for the Modern Art Museum

Shanghai, he made use of outdoor corridors to connect this once closed-off industrial building with the surrounding urban space and rendered it more accessible to the public without sacrificing its historical value. The public nature of these spaces was at the core of the design process from start to finish, helping to turn the river, which has lost its industrial functions over time, into a contemporary urban space that is completely accessible to the public.

Marta Moreira and her MMBB Studio have collaborated with Paulo Mendes da Rocha for many years. In her presentation, Moreira explained how she and Mendes da Rocha turned an abandoned office building into a vibrant community center called SESC-24. Operating under the principles of long-term use and cost effectiveness, they realized their vision for the center through structural renovation, the introduction of footpaths, and an extensive design process that encompassed even the building's tables and chairs. They also added a large rooftop swimming pool, a facility usually only seen in affluent residential neighborhoods, to turn this downtrodden office building into an integrative culture center.

Marcelo Ferraz used the Bread Museum in the small municipality of Ilopolis and the Praca das Artes in the São Paulo city center as examples to illustrate how his studio LTDA creates collective spaces tailored to the needs and interests of residents. Given the importance of European immigration in the history of Ilopolis, Ferraz attempted to incorporate the collective memories of the local immigrant community into the museum's design in the hope that it would become part of the city's public culture. To this end, he analyzed the fundamental structure of European immigrants' dwellings as well as their daily eating habits. By contrast, in São Paulo, he converted a narrow and dreary strip of land separating an industrial and a residential zone into a public urban space that doubles as a formal exhibition center as well as a community venue for artistic activities such as dancing. Through this project, Ferraz strived to create an urban art space that encourages public participation.

In his presentation, Vinicius Andrade shared a unique case: the urban renewal project he planned for an impoverished community on the outskirts of São Paulo. Following a rigorous investigation into the basic local infrastructure such as the state of residences, the waste recycling system, sewage networks and transportation, he proposed an infrastructure-focused renewal plan that would promote a sense of community among locals while leaving them the chance to redefine the space according to their own needs in the future.

Identity: Between Museums and Heritage

Among the projects presented at the forum, buildings with clear cultural implications such as museums, community centers, and exhibition venues accounted for the bulk of case studies. This in itself constitutes an additional typological category: identity. Art historian Louise Noelle Gras believes that this shared pursuit proves that museums and similar institutions are ideal subjects for contemporary architectural experimentation on the theme of modernity; they are "Temples of Modernity." At the same time, in her presentation "A Map, a Conversation, and a Bridge," she delivered a synopsis of how art history has consistently emphasized the notions of globality and interconnectedness. If the field of architecture attributes so much value to museums, it is not only because of their inherent cultural value, their role as landmarks and their public nature—it is also because of their openness and rapid evolution.

In China, exhibition spaces and museums are currently flourishing, while curatorial studies are also entering a stage of increased development. Meanwhile, in Brazil's municipal judicial system, museums belong to a unique category of development encouraged by the government, and as such benefit from

preferential policies such as tax exemptions. This makes them a particularly popular choice in urban renewal initiatives.

In addition to museums, Carlos Eduardo Comas believes that the renewal of heritage architecture is highly valued in contemporary Chinese and Brazilian architectural experimentation. Whether it's the conversion of a concrete factory for the Nanjing Horticultural Expo Park or the renovation of an office building for the SESC-24 community center, it's clear that China and Brazil—two developing nations that have undergone dramatic processes of modernization—are both searching for solutions to problems of conservation and renewal resulting from rapid urbanization. This forum confirmed that China's and Brazil's contemporary architects have stepped into the same battleground; that is, they are all considering the contemporary evolution of heritage from a variety of perspectives, such as ancient engineering wisdom, collective memories, and structural expression.

This China–Brazil Architecture Forum was an innovative, high-level academic event that explored new developments in contemporary architecture from a global perspective. Architectural historian Lu Yongyi commented that the dialogue between Chinese and Brazilian architects has provided Chinese scholars with an important window into contemporary architectural movements abroad. No longer are the researchers limited to history books; instead, they can diversify their understanding of global architectural history through direct exchanges with the international academic community.

International architecture practices and discourse have long been dominated by developed Western nations. Yet in recent years, regionalized research and local in-depth investigations have helped provide a greater range of perspectives on contemporary architecture. The dialogue between China and Brazil has only contributed to this process. In addition to diversifying the communication lines between Chinese architects and the international architectural community, it has provided invaluable insights into the state of contemporary architectural practice in developing nations.

Bibliography

[1] Li Xiangning, Mo Wanli, "'Contemporary Chinese Architecture' from a Global Perspective," *Time + Architecture*, vol. 2 (2018), 15–19.
[2] Zhu Jianfei, "'Frontline Issues' of Architectural History and Theory: China, East Asia, Cultural Plurality and Sociopolitical Theories," *Architectural Journal*, vol. 11 (2015), 12–14.
[3] Yu Yunlong et al., "Revisiting Forgotten Bonds: Architectural Communication Between China and Brazil," *Arquitextos* (2022), 265; G. A. Bailey, "Missionary Art and Architecture of the Society of Jesus between China and Brazil," *The Oxford Handbook of the Jesuits* (Oxford: Oxford University Press, 2019).
[4] Yu Yunlong and Li Xiangning, "Collaborative Modernism: Brazilian Architecture and the Formation of the Estado Novo (1930s–1940s)," *Architectural Journal*, vol. 7 (2019), 109–114.

Modernity Redux: An Introduction to Contemporary Brazilian Architecture

Carlos Eduardo Comas
Professor, Universidade Federal do Rio Grande do Sul, Porto Alegre
Visiting Professor, Tongji University, Shanghai

Modernity has been an ongoing project for Brazilian architects at least since the 1930 Revolution led by Getulio Vargas. Lucio Costa (1902–1998) then became dean of the Escola Nacional de Belas Artes in Rio de Janeiro, the country's cultural capital. Costa asked for a renewal of architecture comparable to the 1920s renewal of literature and the visual arts, mostly based in São Paulo, the country's economic capital, where expatriate Gregori Warchavchik (1896–1972) had already built a few modernist houses. Costa's deanship (1930–1931) and partnership with Warchavchik (1931–1933) were brief. Published texts and designs kept Costa at the forefront.[1]

Hailing Le Corbusier as the Brunelleschi of the machine age, the pioneer behind the Congrès Internationaux d'Architecture Moderne (CIAM, founded 1928)[2] and the form-giver who had fathered the International style (modern architecture according to Philip Johnson and Henry-Russell Hitchcock, 1932),[3] Costa created a Purist stronghold[4] for which he wrote two seminal essays, one of which, "Universidade do Brasil" (1936)[5] corrects and expands the earlier one, "Razões da Nova Arquitetura" (1935).[6] Costa sees modern architecture as the offspring of the Industrial Revolution and the heir to the academic tradition, a diverse and inclusive system founded upon four principles: elemental geometry, supporting structure, space–time tectonics, and business as usual.

Elemental Geometry

The first principle is the concern with the basic geometry of the elements of architecture and composition, with particular interest in the linearity of point supports and the planarity of walls, floors, and roofs. The concern is with planarity and with transparency mix preferred for the ribbon window and the window wall, over openings in walls. In turn, the need to prevent overheating through transparent surfaces and the need for ventilation leads to a multi-layered facade, which updates the Roman *claustra* or screen wall and the Moorish and Iberian *mashrabiya*. Nothing is new about the *brise-soleil* but the term. Sure, modern architecture promotes an anti-historicist purge. It uses abstraction, minimalism, and elementalism to dispose of applied ornament. However, it admits organic ornament that arises from joints between different materials or between units of the same material, the patterns and textures and shadows of stone or tile facings, brickwork, sunlight control devices, and so on, not to mention murals that change the perception of spatial depth. Amédée Ozenfant and Le Corbusier said everything in nature can be reduced to straight and curved lines, and then to cylinders, pyramids, cones, spheres, cubes, and parallelepipeds. These shapes provoke primary sensations that can be modified by patterns over their surfaces.[7] This notion relates to another: abstraction and figuration as the extreme terms of a progression, instead of opposites, demonstrated by Theo van Doesburg in a series that begins with the realistic image of a cow and ends with a composition of rectangles, passing through many levels of stylization.[8]

Supporting Structure

The second principle is the acknowledgment of the limitations and potentials of different structural solutions vis-à-vis the different programmatic requirements of the industrial society. Modern architecture favors an independent skeleton that permits a free plan and a free facade, via floors that have flat undersides and cantilever from a regular grid of point supports. The flat plate slabs in concrete at Le Corbusier's Maison Dom-Ino (1915) make the point. Exposed beams and cantileverless floor slabs look either advanced or rudimentary depending on the spans involved. The Dom-Ino standard, "pancakes on pins" for critic Colin Rowe,[9] and its variations, including cut and perforated floor slabs, suit most building tasks of the industrial society, from multistory office and apartment buildings to factories and community centers. In special situations with requirements either more or less demanding than normal, modern architecture uses arcuated and tensile structures, even structural masonry. Examples include airship hangars featuring parabolic arches (Eugene Freyssinet, Orly, 1916–1923), vaulted churches (Auguste Perret, Notre Dame du Raincy, 1922), vacation houses and low-cost housing with load-bearing walls (Le Corbusier, de Mandrot House, 1931; Costa & Warchavchik, Gamboa apartments, 1931). Academician Quatremère de Quincy argued that the Egyptian cave, the Chinese tent, and the Greek hut are disciplinary archetypes.[10] Mixing structures is quite acceptable. Different types may be superimposed and/or juxtaposed in a single building (Le Corbusier's Palace of the Soviets, 1932; Rentenanstalt Building, 1933; Costa's semidetached housing at Monlevade, 1934). They may distinguish separate buildings of the same complex, like the Aula Magna and the Rectorate in alternative schemes for the Universidade do Brasil campus (Le Corbusier, July 1936; Costa, September 1936). The former would stand on the ground, a tall box on pilotis dominating the setting as serenely as a Greek temple. The latter would rest on the ground, crab-like, absorbing the setting with its exoskeletal frame suspended by steel cables from a parabolic arch, which evokes the flying buttresses and the dramatic expression of

Gothic cathedrals. Le Corbusier was also the Abbot Suger of the machine age. Abbot Suger (1801–1151) is famous for the redesigning of the Saint-Denis Cathedral in France. He is credited with the invention of flying buttresses and the first Gothic construction.

Space–Time Tectonics

The third principle is the attention paid to the multiple alternatives relating tectonic solutions and spatial definition. Modern architecture favors the autonomy of structure with respect to partitioning but admits their integration. Pace Le Corbusier: modern architecture encompasses both the free plan and the cellular plan associated with the superimposition of load-bearing walls. Alongside the mix and counterpoint of curved, orthogonal, oblique, and jagged lines, modern architecture welcomes the pure prism, which exemplifies subtractive compositions, and the play of volumes, which amounts to additive compositions. It accepts the crystalline, classical composition, designed from without and the organic picturesque composition, designed from within. The partial or almost complete exposure of the pilotis allows for the interplay of inside and outside, challenging the plastic values conventionally linked to the tripartite elevation. Roofs may be inclined,

pleated, or bent plates, single pitched, V-shaped like a butterfly, vaulted, etc. They need not be terraces, yet hip and gabled varieties are frowned upon because of their excessive conventionality. Asymmetrical balance and centrifugal composition are preferred to strict axial symmetry and centripetal composition, but the former do not rule out the latter. The choreography of movement through the building may be straightforward or labyrinthine, always a concern whether called *marche* (the academic word) or *promenade* (the Corbusian way). Regarding materiality, modern architecture makes full use of new as well as ancient materials: reinforced concrete, and brick and wood for support and rusticity (Le Corbusier, Maison de Weekend, 1931; Alvar Aalto, Viipuri Library, 1935); silky marble and granite for luxurious cladding (Ludwig Mies van der Rohe, Barcelona Pavilion, 1929; Giuseppe Terragni, Casa del Fascio, 1935). Old processes can be perfected: *cobogós*, machine-made hollow clay or cement blocks for screen walls, patented in Brazil (1929), ventilate and add intricate patterns under the tropical sun (Luiz Nunes, Rural school in Recife, 1934); wattle-and-daub walls are lifted one floor to escape the humid ground and reinforced with sawn wood to facilitate and speed construction (Costa, semidetached housing at Monlevade, 1934). Modern architecture takes advantage of both industrialization and handicraft. Indeed, standardization of building components is not a modern invention.

Business As Usual

The fourth principle is the reassertion of the utilitarian and representational requirements in architecture against surrender to Fordism and the understanding of the profession as mere service. Architecture, says Costa, is construction with plastic intention, whether conscious, as is proper of erudite art, or unconscious, as in popular art. Firmness and commodity do not dictate form in its entirety, and the sensibility of the architect is always called to intervene and choose between equivalent alternatives. Otherwise, correct composition is not enough to achieve quality in architecture. It must show the distinctive physiognomy of time and place, the proper character of program and situation. The academic tradition had codified the basic characterization strategy long ago, the reference to relevant precedents that evoke a lineage and create a suitable environmental mood. Modern architecture did not change this. It has an iconography. It is indebted to abstract art, fast vehicles, timeless popular architecture, engineering feats, and utilitarian construction; at the same time it renews old metaphors connecting architecture to the human body and to Noah's ark, columns to trees. Modern architecture, Costa writes, is a smart girl with no make-up and spindly legs—amid Rio's alleys lined with imperial palms that Le Corbusier found fascinating. Modern architecture is neither a question of iconolatry nor iconoclasm. But allusion is always preferable to citation and replication, much as polite but lively conversation is always preferable to grandiloquent speech.

Cariocas and Paulistas

From the late 1930s to the early 1980s, in the aftermath of the international oil crisis and the end of the Brazilian economic "miracle," when critics such as Charles Jencks proclaimed that modern architecture was dead, those principles informed the work of three successive groups of practitioners, all of them trained at least partially under the Beaux-Arts academic system. The oldest group comprises those who came of age professionally in the late 1930s, foremost among them the Cariocas (those who were born or living in Rio) Costa, Luiz Nunes, Marcelo and Milton Roberto, Oscar Niemeyer, Jorge Moreira, and Affonso Eduardo Reidy, as well as the Paulistas (born or living in São Paulo) Warchavchik and Rino Levi. A second group followed, those who came of age in the 1950s, such as Paulistas Vilanova Artigas and Lina Bo Bardi, and Carioca Sergio Bernardes. Those who came of age in the 1960s include Paulistas Paulo Mendes da Rocha, Joaquim Guedes, Carlos Millan, and Jerônimo Bonilha Esteves, and Rio-educated Marcos Konder Neto, Lelé Filgueras Lima, Severiano Porto, and Luiz Paulo Conde. Collaborators included master landscape architect Roberto Burle Marx and first-rate engineers like Emilio Baumgart, Joaquim Cardozo, and João Carlos Figueiredo Ferraz. The work of the period can conveniently be divided into two partially overlapping episodes.

The earlier episode is linked with a Rio-based Carioca school. Its ways supplanted the Purist or International Style explorations in the country, including most but not all of the designs done by Costa until 1936. Although remaining a minority affair, the Carioca school had the strong support of Gustavo Capanema, Vargas' Minister of Education, and from Juscelino Kubitschek, then mayor of Belo Horizonte, the capital of an important province. Vargas' deposition in 1945 did not affect the school's standing. Triumphing over historicist eclecticism and Colonial-style revivalism, the Carioca ways became hegemonic all over the country at the beginning of the Cold War and marched toward apotheosis and twilight with the competition for the Pilot Plan of the new capital Brasília (1957), an initiative of then president Kubitschek, half-built when inaugurated (1960). Those ways became dated—though not dead, despite the early passing of leaders such as Marcelo and Milton Roberto and Reidy—by the mid-1960s, while Brasília was being consolidated, under military rule since the right-wing 1964 Revolution. The second episode is linked with a São Paulo–based school, which emerged around 1960. The Paulista ways became hegemonic in the mid-1960s, becoming dated by the late 1970s.

Metapurism and Brutalism

Metapurism—beyond purism—seems an adequate label for the work of the Carioca school,[11] as it sided with Le Corbusier (but also Mies, Aalto, and Terragni) in the effort to overcome the limitations of the white boxes associated with Purism and the International style. Metapurism developed in three phases: aspirant, dominant, and mutant. The milestones of the school's initial decade are celebrated in *Brazil Builds: Architecture New and Old, 1652–1942*,[12] the widely diffused catalog of the exhibition at MoMA. Brazil is one of the protagonists of *Latin American Architecture since 1945*,[13] another MoMA catalog, but the true sequel is *Modern Architecture in Brazil*,[14] not to mention several special issues of journals like *Progressive Architecture, Architectural Forum,*

The Architectural Review, and *L'Architecture d'Aujourd'hui*. After the second decade came the design and construction of the Brasília palaces, churches, and university buildings, when Niemeyer's aesthetics inflect as he and his collaborators deal with monumentality and prefabrication. Brasília was the object of worldwide scrutiny and criticism, which became demonization after the military seized power and saw to the completion of the city's federal government sector in the mid-1970s.

Brutalist is the usual label for the work of the Paulista school, but Reidy's Museum of Modern Art in Rio (designed 1953, first block completed 1957, second block completed 1967) anticipates its ways, and its emergence parallels the design and construction of Rio's Monument to the Dead of World War II by Marcos Konder Neto and Helio Ribas (1957–1959), as well as Niemeyer's buildings in Brasília. Maybe mutant Metapurism is to be seen as Protobrutalism. The Brutalist ways were identified with São Paulo in Brazilian historiography, even though they became hegemonic all over the country in the late 1960s. Their development was practically unnoticed by critics in the developed world. The Brazil Pavilion by Mendes da Rocha at Expo 70 in Osaka did not get any attention, either at the time or in the textbooks published in the following decade, contrary to what had

happened regarding the Brazil Pavilion by Costa and Niemeyer at the New York's World Fair of 1939, or even the Brazil Pavilion by Bernardes at Expo 58 in Brussels.

Carioca Basics/Programs and Sites

The early Carioca work uses reinforced concrete "pancakes on pins," except for fair pavilions in steel, some country inns using wood poles, and houses done in structural masonry. Walls are usually made of hollow clay bricks, plastered and painted. Window walls coexist with ribbon windows and holes in walls. Facings and claddings vary according to occasion and situation, contributing to the maximalist materiality. The palette includes stone, mosaic tiles, factory-made and hand-painted azulejos, satiny and glossy metal sheets, wood in many guises, as well as asbestos cement and clay roof tiles. Equally prized, curves and straight lines appear either singly or combined in the elements of architecture and composition. Columns are circular. Pillars are square. H-steel profiles get a metal cladding. Wood poles are left untreated. Multistory compositions are normally tripartite, additive, and asymmetrically balanced. The formal distinction of the elements of composition is both pragmatic and symbolic.

Bodies in those compositions hold repetitive, generic program requirements. The standard *parti* is easy to describe. Elongated boxes with blank end walls (for bracing) and glazed front and rear (for light and lightness) stand on differentiated bases and crowns, while inner and/or outer service cores provide additional bracing. The vertical continuity of the blank facades is stressed by downplaying the external register of the floor slabs. Bent, elongated boxes relate to topography and situation. Sunscreens or sun breakers intensify the contrast between facades, which go from smooth to grainy to layered, featuring striated, gridded, or trellised screens, from transparent to lacy to opaque. Texture contributes to the virtual decomposition of the built volume into its constituent planes. Contrasts feed other debates as well, between volumetric containment and sprawl, stratification and verticality, tautness and looseness, not to mention the irregular disposition of walls and the regular grid of supports. Despite the foundational role attributed to structure, walls and supports have the same rank as elements of architecture and composition.

Bases and crowns accommodate special, singular program requirements. Bases rise from artificial ground treated as garden and/ or platform. They often present volumes contained within the limits of the ground-floor pilotis and volumes expanding under or beyond the cantilevered bodies. Inside and outside interweave progressively. Bases are porous, with intermediate voids that serve as porticos and open public passages. Movement through them becomes an elaborate promenade. The partial suppression of cantilevers allows for point supports that emulate a colossal order. A favorite motif for the bases of corporate and government buildings, colossal columns combine with double-height columns to suggest dignity without grandiloquence, while downplaying mezzanines. Bases of apartment buildings usually feature single-height point supports. Gravity is challenged in both cases, and the body of the building compares to a balloon ready to leave ground. Crowns add to the formal diversity, appearing as stepped volumes, walled gardens, penthouses with cantilevered pergolas, partially built-up terraces, and monopitch or V-shaped ("butterfly") roofs, sometimes tiled. Vaulted roofs over auditoriums, factories, and warehouses introduce structural diversity.

Besides vaulted roofs, special structures include vaults rising from the ground to define a church—suggesting bent floor slabs—and glued wood arches doing the same in a tractor showroom. Mixing structures is a common practice. In both cases, they cover independent and shorter mezzanines on a reinforced concrete pilotis. Cantileverless, exoskeletal frames appear in theaters and gymnasiums, their columns tapering down, crab-like. Regarding iconography, allusions to the baroque and neoclassical Brazilian past are as obvious as allusions to the country's vernacular buildings, hilly topography, and picturesque squares and parks. In hindsight, connections with the classical tradition are equally strong. Moreover, there are nods to the abstract expressionism of Joan Miró and Jean Arp, as well as stylized evocations of naval architecture. Archetypes are duly honored. Typological exploration comprises both building and open spaces. Designing the modern square or park is as important as designing the modern monument.

Carioca Dominance and Mutation

The range of programs and sites of early Carioca work is impressive. It includes mid- and high-rises with clear, representational requirements for government and corporate headquarters, apartment buildings, housing schemes, hotels, buildings for "cultivating the body and the spirit," technical schools, and a few houses and warehouses. Sites went from whole blocks in downtown or suburbs, to small lots in old neighborhoods. In the postwar period, from the mid-1940s to the mid-1950s, commissions for upscale apartment and office buildings increased, along with demands for hotels, hospitals, and houses. The results were less praised than the social housing schemes and less prestigious than the newly founded museums or Niemeyer's exceptional complex of exhibition halls and assorted facilities at the Ibirapuera in São Paulo. The complex is an additive composition that features a huge forest-like, free-form connecting element, a covered plaza known locally as the Ibirapuera marquee, whose floor slopes, accompanying the topography. The same idea is applied to the ground-floor shopping area of multifunctional complexes in downtown São Paulo. Interplay of outside and inside acquires other meaning in work that belies the monofunctional zoning promoted by the CIAM Athens Charter (1933).

Importance of Ramps and the Choreography of Movement

Innovations of the early and mid-1950s deserve recognition. Bent, elongated boxes of superblock length characterize spectacular housing schemes that respond to the topography of their sites, whether centrally located sloping terrain or peripheric hillsides. Sometimes the exposed pilotis migrates to or reappears in the floor above the rooftop terrace of an expanded base. The so-called "free-form" floor or roof slab is found in houses and apartment buildings. Uprights with brackets are reminiscent of tree trunks like the V- and W-shaped columns that increase spans at the ground floor, irrespectively of program. The demand for higher levels of service and flexibility in commercial buildings and museums led to fewer point supports and bigger spans, which made waffle and ribbed floor slabs a common feature. Exoskeletal frames are exploited in diverse types of exhibition spaces and the occasional factory. The profile of the exposed beams of those frames may be boomerang-shaped or simply oblique, instead of horizontal, while the columns are plates tapering down as thick as the beams. At their most developed, at the Museum of Modern Art, exoskeletal columns have an asymmetrical V-shape, and steel cables suspended from the exoskeletal beams support an intermediary floor slab. Steel tensile structures distinguish temporary exhibition pavilions and the marquees of permanent grandstands. Materiality remains maximalist.

Partis became more compact in monumental Brasília, abundantly photographed even if maligned. It will suffice here to reiterate that innovations include figural peristyles with columns tapering upwards and downwards, which surround glass boxes without sunshades, and cantileverless floor slabs with the thinnest edges coexist with hypercantilevers in the smaller facades. The marble-clad columns of the presidential residence have been described as modern, bulging caryatids. Those of the presidential workplace have been described as modern, graceful atlantes. Forceful geometry and opacity characterize the Assembly Halls of the National Congress, the National Theater, and the Cathedral. Steel is used for the Telecommunications Tower—in combination with massive V-shaped pylons—and for all ministries except justice and foreign affairs.

The love of beauty turns into an appetite for the sublime, although the architecture in Brasília is less exuberant than in Rio. Experiences with prefabrication at the Bus Terminal Platform and the University of Brasília's buildings— including a curvaceous, superblock length Central Institute of Sciences—awaken the passion for raw concrete already seen in Rio's Museum of Modern Art and Monument to the Dead of World War II. The latter's crypt features remarkable sculptural columns with anthropomorphic connotations, the intersection of a pyramid tapering up, and a rectangular trapezoid tapering down suggesting a phalanx of warriors.

Paulista Basics

The Paulista work celebrates engineering by means of a few formally assertive supports beneath hypercantilevered boxes, cantileverless boxes, or a combination of both—along with ribbed or waffle slabs endowed with skylights on occasion, plus ducts and cables exposed as emblems of honesty. Walls and sunshade devices are subordinated or integrated to the reinforced concrete frame. Compact partis parallel the palaces of Brasília. Interplay between inside and outside goes on. Compositions emphasize elevational bipartition, a transparent base beneath an opaque box. The box ranges from a big, sheltering, thick roof slab to a tower; one-story-high boxes are mainly domestic, called house-apartments because their ground floors open for entrance and services; and two- to three-story-high boxes are institutional. "Few supports" means massive or wide supports. Supports at the ground level may be thick cylindrical columns, cuboid pillars, or pyramids tapering up with metal or rubber joints between them and the box above. Alternatively, they may be blade-like, with the thickness of walls or beams, and taper down either perpendicular to the facade plane of the box or prolonging that plane. Sometimes they meet blade-like or pyramidal lower supports that taper up, and their combination generates a colossal column and amplifies their anthropomorphic connotations. Exotic peristyles go hand-in-hand with the big roof. The opposition between blank and glazed facades remains a trend, with curtain walls replacing window walls, and some examples of prefabricated load-bearing concrete panels incorporating windows. These create facade grids usually resting on transfer beams supported by a few thick pillars at the base, the blank end panels rising from ground to top. On the whole, the body of the building now compares mainly to a stone chunk falling from the sky and held aloft with effort. Gravity is intensified rather than defied. Crowns are downplayed, reduced to an edge or parapet.

If "pancakes on pins" remains the standard structure, houses sometimes sport barrel-vaulted roofs, defining cellular plans or parabolic vaults rising from the ground that could be erected first, further construction proceeding in a dry setting. For a while these vaults were prefabricated as arcuated hollow clay-block slabs. Prefabrication justified many design decisions, as it was deemed emblematic of industrialization and socioeconomic development. Nevertheless, orthogonality was not a fetish. Besides being present in tapering supports, obliques also feature in ramps that articulate binuclear plans and reiterate the importance of architectural elements in the choreography of movement in the Paulista spaces. Then, curves are episodic and mostly regular, although they shape not only beautiful staircases and the four spectacular banana-like branches of the Jahu Bus Terminal pillars, but also the circular Paulistano gymnasium atop a rectangular base. The gym resembles an X-ray of the Chamber of Deputies in Brasília. The reinforced concrete superstructure over the base's roof terrace comprises a ring-shaped roof slab that connects six radial plates tapering down and up. Steel cables are anchored in those plates' upper section, above the roof slab, and they suspend the center of the sports court's circular metallic roof, while the external edge of this roof rests on the inner edge of the concrete ring. Last, but not least, Paulistas do not hesitate to use load-bearing masonry, wood poles, and tiled roofs in beach houses.

Variety matters in an approach to architecture that values rough tactility and strong minimalist impulses. Formwork made of wood planks results in raw concrete surfaces left unpainted. The symbolic connotations of concrete almost surpass its practical qualities. Exposed brick makes an appearance. Facings are almost nonexistent, although plastered masonry is accepted, and contrasts are created by floors featuring tiles in intricate nineteenth-century patterns, waxed hardwood boards, or satiny stone. Unframed tempered glass panes add glitter. To be clear, this is arte povera by intention, not by lack of means.

Contrasts and Affinities

Both the Carioca and the Paulista schools were progressive. They defended industrialization and the industrial society. They believed that socioeconomic development was tied to state or liberal capitalism, and large techno-bureaucracies. A better tomorrow required big plans and a top-down approach, even if it relied on support by the people. However, epicurean grace characterizes even severe Carioca work, and stoic severity characterizes even graceful Paulista work. Rio extending into Brasília favors smoothness, transparency, thinness, upward lightness, gloss, shallowness, and painterliness, although it is not averse to the rustic. São Paulo is always partial to rusticity, cultivating roughness, opacity, and thickness, although it is not averse to a touch of glitter. The Paulista work exudes a downward heaviness and minimizes supports. It favors matte surfaces, depth, and sculptural effects. The elimination of facings

and postproduction finishing of the elements of architecture accompanies the use of fewer supports and big, clear spans. Paulista architects often fuse structure with external walls or fixed sunbreakers, while autonomous walls and structure have equal rank in Carioca compositions. Carioca work highlights ephemerality; São Paulo bets on eternity.

Nevertheless, correspondences between São Paulo and Brasília should not be discounted. Work in the new capital both anticipates and parallels the Paulista Brutalism. For instance, Rio favors expansive compositions, while São Paulo and Brasília favor volumetric compactness; the primacy of structure, the assimilation of supports to walls, and the demise of mobile sunbreakers is as evident in the palaces or the university buildings of Brasília as in São Paulo. Correspondences can also be found in design ethos. Epicurean, in the proper sense of the word, means "moderate, open, and balanced." It relates to ethics as much as stoicism. At its best, Rio balanced the Vitruvian triad of *firmitas*, *commoditas*, and *venustas*. Some aspects of commoditas were notoriously sacrificed to representation in São Paulo as in Brasília, although with different connotations. Comfort was considered bourgeois in São Paulo, and it may have taken second place, after speed of construction, in Brasília. In both cities, exaggeration took

command. São Paulo is not the antithesis of the Carioca school, Brasília is not simply Rio's extension, and only hegemonic Metapurism and Brutalism can be accurately described as national phenomena.

Contemporary Modern

Niemeyer and Lelé did not cease to work when the Carioca school faded. Mendes da Rocha, Bo Bardi, and Guedes did not stop designing architecture in the mid-1970s as the economy slowed down, or in the mid-1980s, which saw the re-democratization of Brazil as a necessary step for economic recovery. Indeed, except for Bo Bardi, who died in 1992, they kept working well into the twenty-first century. Moreover, a new group of practitioners entered the professional scene, those who had been trained under modern architecture and came of age in the 1970s and the 1980s, among them Marcos Acayaba, Isay Weinfeld, and Marcio Kogan from São Paulo; Hector Vigliecca and Bruno Padovano, Eolo Maia, and Sylvio Podestá from Minas Gerais; Carlos Nelson Ferreira dos Santos and Claudio Bernardes from Rio; and Sergio Magalhães. Very few fell for idealist postmodernism, either neo-rationalist (the Aldo Rossi kind) or minimalist (the Tadao Ando sort), and even fewer fell for historicist postmodernism, either free classicist (the

Michael Graves manner) or deconstructivist (the Rem Koolhaas way).

Maybe that happened because of the sheer brilliance of the late work of Bo Bardi and Mendes da Rocha. Maybe that happened because a historiographic revision was establishing the richness of Brazilian modern architecture in sounder terms and rightly emphasizing its diversity while showing that the relationship of modern architecture to context and history was much richer than even admirers recognized. As outlined by Costa, its principles admitted both/and as well as either/or, and that was decades before *Complexity and Contradiction in Architecture*[15] sang the praises of ambivalence. Speaking to both educated and lay people using stylization was double-coding decades before *The Language of Postmodern Architecture*[16] praised it. At their best, Cariocas and Paulistas, Metapurists, and Brutalists were imaginative realists, trying to get maximal returns out of scarce resources. They were not utopians. They neither thought that the industrial society was paradise, nor idealized the agrarian past. Interest in advanced construction technology and prefabrication did not rule out interest in improving low technology and promoting the rationalization of production. Their idea of the age as a palimpsest has not aged. They would better be described as critical internationalists, the term

coined by French historian Jean-Louis Cohen.[17] They had common sense, these progressivists, who could, when needed, act as culturalists.

Architects that came of age in the 1990s also embraced modern architecture as a living tradition. That group includes Marcelo Ferraz (Brasil Arquitetura), Thiago Bernardes, Marta Moreira (MMBB Arquitetos), Angelo Bucci (SPBR Arquitetos), Vinicius Andrade, and Marcelo Morettin (Andrade Morettin), Fernanda Barbara, and Fabio Valentim, as well as Cristiane Muniz and Felipe Viegas (UNA), and Martin Corullon (Metro Arquitetos), many of whom collaborated with Bo Bardi and Mendes da Rocha. In hindsight, as far as Brazil is concerned, the 1980s separate a historic or vintage modern architecture from a contemporary modern architecture that thrives to this day.

One lacks perspective to define more precisely such contemporary architecture, although it can be said that it corresponds to a postmodern historical condition as lived in an emerging country of the Global South and that São Paulo is its epicenter. No doubt that the late works of Bo Bardi and Mendes da Rocha are its most important beacons to date. One can say that contemporary modern architecture in Brazil opens with the completion of the SESC Pompeia Cultural Center (Bo Bardi with

Ferraz and André Vainer, 1975–1986) and peaks with the completion of the SESC 24 de maio Cultural Center (Mendes da Rocha with MMBB, 2002–2017). Social condensers in hot and cool versions respectively, involving the adaptive reuse of a factory in the first case and a department store in the second, they testify to the importance that remodeling of ordinary buildings is assumed to be an architectural problem. Besides its positive implications regarding sustainability of the built environment, it advances the idea of architecture as palimpsest, in which new and old elements coexist in stimulating tension—old not being necessarily identified as a precious antique. All things considered, the architectural work with artistic pretentions of these three decades has focused on subtle evolution rather than formal breakthroughs, quality rather than innovation, consistency rather than pyrotechnics. Free-form concrete seems a thing of the past, as the increasing availability of structural steel and new developments in wood technology promote restraint in design. For better or worse, Niemeyer's exuberance is not a source of inspiration. Understatement is the name of the game. As Mies once said, one does not need a new architecture every Monday.[18] As in the past, there is more to Brazilian modern architecture than meets the eye.

[1] For a detailed analysis of Brazilian modern architecture, see Carlos Eduardo Comas, *Précisions brésiliennes sur un état passé de l'architecture et de l'urbanisme modernes d'après les projets et les ouvrages de Lucio Costa, Oscar Niemeyer, MM Roberto, Affonso Reidy, Jorge Moreira & Cie., 1936–1945* (PhD dissertation, Université de Paris VIII, 2002); Ruth Verde Zein, A arquitetura da escola paulista brutalista (PhD dissertation, UFRGS, 2006); Carlos Eduardo Comas, "Notes on two Brazilian schools," *Latin America in Construction, 1955–1980* (New York: MoMA, 2015).

[2] Eric Mumford, *The CIAM Discourse on Urbanism, 1928–1960* (Cambridge, Mass.: 2000).

[3] Henry-Russell Hitchcock and Philip Johnson, *The International Style* (New York: MoMA, 1932).

[4] Lucio Costa, "Depoimento de um arquiteto carioca," *Sobre arquitetura* (Porto Alegre: CEUA, 1962), 192.

[5] Lucio Costa, "Universidade do Brasil," *Sobre arquitetura* (Porto Alegre: CEUA, 1962).

[6] Lucio Costa, "Razões da nova arquitetura," *Sobre arquitetura* (Porto Alegre: CEUA, 1962).

[7] Amédée Ozenfant and Le Corbusier, "Sur la plastique," L'Esprit Nouveau 1 (1920), 38–48. The article echoes Piet Mondrian, "Dialog on the New Plastic," *De Stijl* (February–March 1919), in Harry Holtzman and Martin S. James (eds. and trans.), *The New Art – The New Life: The Collected Writings of Piet Mondrian* (New York: Da Capo Press, 1993), 77.

[8] Theo van Doesburg, *The Cow* (1918). https://www.khanacademy.org/humanities/art-1010/cubism-early-abstraction/de-stijl/a/de-stijl-part-ii-near-abstraction-and-pure-abstraction

[9] Colin Rowe. *The Mathematics of the Ideal Villa and Other Essays* (Cambridge, Mass.: MIT, 1976), 196.

[10] A-C Quatremère de Quincy, *De l'architecture égyptienne considérée dans son origine, ses principes et son goût, et comparée sous les mêmes rapports à l'architecture grecque* (Paris: Barrois, 1803).

[11] Kenneth Frampton, *Modern Architecture: A Critical History* (London: Thames and Hudson, 1980), 254. Frampton sees Brazilian modern architecture (i.e., the Carioca school) as a transformation of Corbusian Purist components.

[12] Philip L. Goodwin and G. E. Kidder Smith, *Brazil Builds: Architecture New and Old, 1652–1942* (New York: MoMA, 1942).

[13] Henry-Russell Hitchcock, *Latin American Architecture since 1945* (New York: MoMA, 1955).

[14] Henrique Mindlin, *Modern Architecture in Brazil* (Amsterdam: Colibris, 1956).

[15] Robert Venturi Jr, *Complexity and Contradiction in Architecture* (New York: MoMA, 1966).

[16] Charles Jencks, *The Language of Postmodern Architecture* (London: Academy Editions, 1977).

[17] Jean-Louis Cohen, *The Future of Architecture Since 1889: A Worldwide History* (London: Phaidon, 2016).

[18] Quoted in Peter Carter, *Mies at Work* (London: Phaidon, 1999).

A Verandah Conversation

David Leatherbarrow
Emeritus Professor, School of Design, University of Pennsylvania
Foreign Dean, IDS, Southeast University

This short report replaces a scholarly study of the distinct conceptions of modern architecture held by architects in different parts of the world: Brazil, China, and the United States. That study was put aside because of the importance of the recent discovery of a conversation between three key figures in this interchange: Lucio Costa, Yang Tingbo, and Paul Philippe Cret. The chance meeting of these three will strike many readers as hardly credible, but that doubt doesn't diminish its intrinsic interest.

An anonymous transcription of a conversation between three modern architects has very recently come into the possession of a newly retired professor living in Philadelphia. The interlocutors were from widely different parts of the world: Brazil, China, and the United States. Because no record of the meeting can be found in existing scholarship, many readers will wonder if it really occurred. Broadly speaking, their friendly afternoon discussion addressed the prospects of modern architecture in their home locations. As if for the benefit of contemporary readers, the similarities and differences of their viewpoints offer a strikingly nuanced view of architectural modernism as a historical, geographical, and cultural practice. The dialogue's rather direct bearing on current thinking will also be clear.

Locations always hold secrets, for scholars no less than for designers. The professor who chanced upon the transcription happens to live on a short street named Woodland Terrace in Philadelphia, a street that edges two important elements of the city's topography: a trolley station and a cemetery; the first is evidence of the city's twentieth-century modernization, and the second of its desire to keep its past present. A window in the professor's library faces the house where the conversation took place, an urban villa from 1861, which was for several decades the residence of the famous French-American architect, author, and professor Paul Philippe Cret. Apparently, the transcript was found during a period of house clearing and later shared with the professor who lives across the street. Although Cret was nearly deaf in his senior years, the house was something of a salon in 1920s and 1930s, thanks in a large part to Madam Cret, whose grace and modest sophistication impressed all who enjoyed her parties—architects, musicians, artists, and scholars. But the communication that concerns us did not take place during a party, not even inside the house; instead, it was on the house's front verandah, in view of both the graves and the trollies, those emblems of the past and present.

Woodland Terrace, Philadelphia, Paul Philippe Cret's house, view from study toward the verandah
©David Leatherbarrow

Woodland Terrace, Philadelphia
©David Leatherbarrow

Woodland Avenue Trolley and Woodland Cemetery, Philadelphia
©David Leatherbarrow

Woodland Terrace, Philadelphia, verandah with Paul Philippe
Cret historic marker
©David Leatherbarrow

Benjamin Franklin Parkway, Philadelphia, view toward City Hall
©David Leatherbarrow

The happy accident of crossed paths happened as follows. One of Cret's former students, Yang Tingbo, classmate and friend of Louis I. Kahn, rather unexpectedly returned to Philadelphia in 1939. Who knows what urgent business took him back to the US, perhaps it was something to do with the Sino-Japanese War, then making life in China miserable. Existing records of Yang's life contain no evidence of this unexpected visit, and it is likely that present-day historians will label this account fictious.

Like any former student who comes to the city of an admired teacher, this one didn't miss the chance to surprise the old professor with a call at his home. He hadn't been there often, but knew the place, having resided in university dormitories a couple of blocks away (next to the site where Kahn would build his famous Richards Medical Center). But when the door to his professor's house opened, Yang was surprised when it was Madam Cret who greeted him, and took him into the large front room. For there, sitting across from the professor was another unexpected guest, a famous architect from Brazil, Lucio Costa, who had, on that same day, stopped in Philadelphia en route to New York City, where he was working with Oscar Niemeyer on the Brazil Pavilion for the World's Fair. Many things attracted Lucio to Philadelphia: Cret's work, the PSFS building of Howe and Lescaze, and the city itself, though here, too, no existing biographies mention this visit, suggesting again the fabricated nature of this report. Still, we should imagine Lucio in Cret's house, soon to meet and spend time on the verandah with an equally distinguished visitor from China.

After awkward but well-intentioned greetings, the two visitors immediately found themselves in agreement about the pleasure of seeing examples of the professor's recent work. They were in luck, for he happened to have at home drawings of a cemetery gateway he had just designed for the entry on the other side of Woodland Avenue, 50 meters from his house. In six years' time, Cret himself would be

Paul Philippe Cret, Woodland Cemetery gateway, Philadelphia
©David Leatherbarrow

Woodland Cemetery tombs, Philadelphia
©David Leatherbarrow

buried there. Confident that better light would help them see the drawings, the professor proposed they relocate to the front verandah. Once seated, but before Tingbo and Lucio had enough time with the elevations and details, the professor proposed yet another move, this time to the actual site of his project. Attractive as the verdant, monument-filled landscape seemed from a distance, Cret advised against going past the gate, for the tomb architecture was excessively eclectic, hardly the sense of history he advocated. Tingbo also turned away, though he didn't mention his own battles with the Chinese equivalent to this historicism in Shanghai and other places that coupled misunderstood motifs from both the West and China. Lucio didn't comment, but his agreement was silently understood. The nearby trolleys, of course, indicated the opposite approach to design, taking the lead from contemporary technology. Public transportation would be less important than motorways in Lucio's not-yet-designed Brasília, but his task of reconciling modern methods with civic values would also position design between interests that seemed entirely opposed. Cret's designs for train cars involved reduced ornament, but also well-proportioned surfaces, as did his design for these gates—classical and modern, anticipating, one might say, the work of his other student, Louis I. Kahn, Tingbo's friend. Lucio, however, asked the professor about the one representational figure that did appear on the gates: a winged hourglass. Before the professor could reply, Tingbo proposed a disciplinary interpretation: architecture's task is to find new ways to keep the past present. In his explanation, however, the professor first cited Shakespeare: time's "swiftest hours," then Alexander Pope, in life "swiftly fly the years." Lucio's cultural background allowed him to name the ancient source: Virgil's *tempus fugit*.

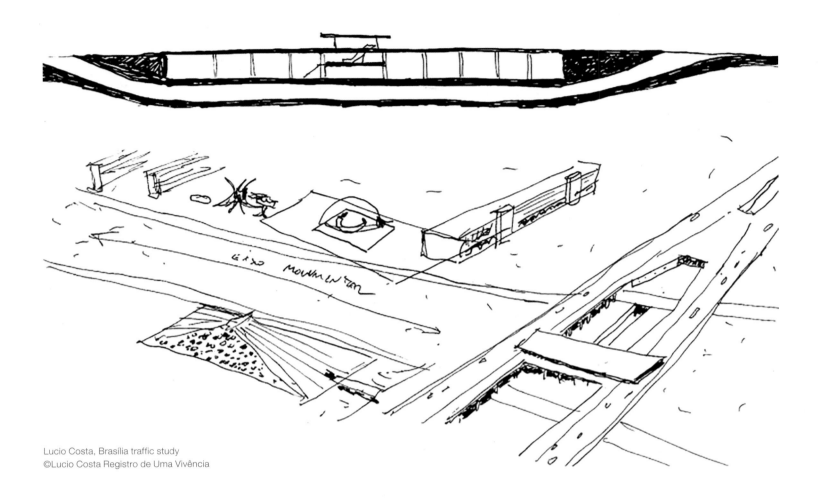

Lucio Costa, Brasília traffic study
©Lucio Costa Registro de Uma Vivência

Paul Philippe Cret, Woodland Cemetery gate emblem, Philadelphia
©David Leatherbarrow

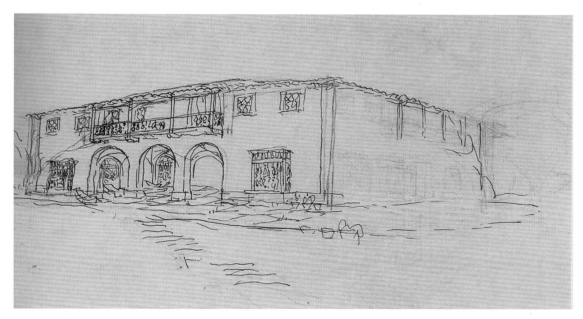

Lucio Costa, vernacular studies
©Lucio Costa Registro de Uma Vivência

Once they returned to the verandah, the professor asked Lucio why the emblem caught his attention. His reply was that the problem of historical continuity was very much on his mind. It was also, he explained, a concern for other Brazilian modernists in Rio, São Paulo, and other cities from Recife down to Porto Alegre. Two years earlier he had started work on a museum of artifacts collected from the many Jesuit missions built in the Brazilian interior in the seventeenth and eighteenth centuries. The museum's site, in clear view of the broken body of the São Miguel church, bordered an excavated village and monastic precinct. He explained: "I wanted to build at the edge of the ancient square a simple refuge for pieces that would gain much from being assessed in direct contact with the rest of the ruins." Though he intended the attached gatekeeper's house to "evoke ancient porticoes," he tried his best, he said, "to avoid reproduction." His pavilion will never fall victim to that accusation, for it is basically a glass diaphragm under a solid roof: lightweight, fully transparent at its sides, expressing a modern sensibility in both its materials and spatial qualities. "Transparency," Lucio told his new friends, was "a modern means of disclosing the several layers of a site's historical past—not only colonial, also European, and native or indigenous." In Brazil, it seems, the historical problem for modern architects was to address several distinct periods and peoples, with no illusions about mono-ethnic origins, still less, a single authentic way of building. If the nucleus of creative production is found in inherited culture, Brazil's is irreducibly composite. That's no less true today than in the 1930s.

Lucio Costa, São Miguel Museu das Missões
©David Leatherbarrow

Lucio Costa, São Miguel Museu das Missões, interior
©David Leatherbarrow

Yang Tingbo, Music Stage, Nanjing
©David Leatherbarrow

Tingbo explained that the problem in China is different, given the long continuity of the people in the place, and its comparative isolation until the modern period. He neglected to mention the unequal sizes of the different ethnic groups, the Han people being the largest. The Chinese conversation involved an exchange between modern (or modernizing) culture and an ancient, compact, and still venerable past. A case in point, he explained with pride that wasn't entirely concealed, was a music stage he had completed seven years earlier in Nanjing on Purple Mountain, which was home to a large and increasing number of important tombs and memorials, more historicist than eclectic (in the sense of the cemetery they had just glimpsed), though over-scaled and un-apologetically deceptive with respect to actual structure. One example would be the Sun Yat-sen Museum, next to which his project had been sited.

If traditionalism is the dead faith of the living, authentic tradition is the living faith of the dead. Here, too, original impulses were nameless. Looking at Cret, as if to repeat something he'd learnt as a student, Tingbo said, "[In China] we appreciate tradition's spirit, not only its form." The matter seemed both disciplinary and cultural. Shifting from tradition to style, he observed: "Style is an odd thing, it cultivates people's impressions, hobbies, and habits, and endows architecture with a regional character … Style and form are the reason architecture appeals to people. [But once styles] are formed people worship them."

Lucio replied that was the risk and architects are normally punished for their good deeds. As a serious look replaced his affirmative smile, Tingbo then shifted to the problem of work at any historical moment, not only theirs: "The culture of architecture represents its epoch …

during my study [with Professor Cret] the application of new structures, materials, and techniques forced [us] to seek new possibilities for architecture."

At this turn in the conversation Cret reminded Tingbo of what he'd taught about the design of bridges, the one on the river side of the cemetery they had just seen, for example. The problem of form and technique is a big challenge because "the old unity between architecture and engineering has been severed … they have become individual [even] impenetrable to one another, yet [they are and must be] indissolubly connected, for good or ill."

Sun Yat-Sen Mausoleum, Nanjing
©David Leatherbarrow

Yang Tingbo, music stage upper walk, Nanjing
©David Leatherbarrow

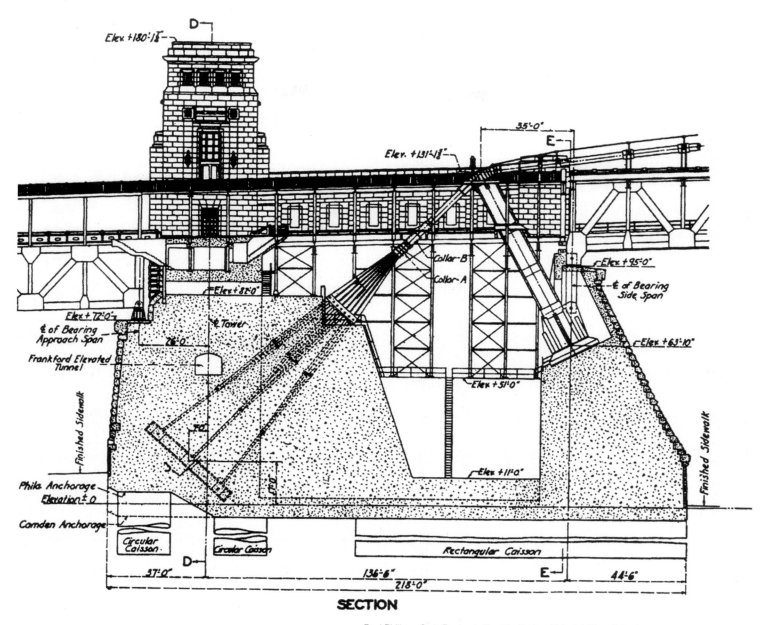

SECTION

Paul Philippe Cret, Benjamin Franklin Bridge, Philadelphia, reinforcing in the abutment, section
©University of Pennsylvania Libraries

Lucio, with an abruptness that was uncharacteristic, interrupted with a question: "Why ill?" Noticing the surprise of his new friends, he continued more calmly, asking about an element like the lattice screen, versions of which can be seen in Brazil and Portugal, but also Egypt, and even China. For him, it seemed the issue was two-part: every form suits a recognizable purpose, but materials and techniques of construction inevitably change. One suspects he was thinking of the facade screen in his New York pavilion. He and Oscar wanted their building in New York "to be a simple, rather informal, attractive and welcoming pavilion, one that imposed itself neither for its size, for the site is not big, nor its lavishness, as the country is still poor, but for its harmony and balance, and as an expression … of contemporary art." The honeycombed facade of his competition entry evolved into the sculptural alveolar diaphragm of the final design—a sibling form to both the traditional *cobogo* screens and the recent design by Luis Nunes for the water tower on the Olinda hill in Recife. But what had been hand-made timber construction of lattices in past architectures became ceramic or concrete in modern buildings. Instead of saying more about the projects, or anticipating what he would build at Parque Guinle, he offered Tingbo and the professor a statement of principle: "[Architects] with a truly modern spirit have found a fundamental discord between present building processes and the historical styles and [therefore must] seek to readjust those processes away from the dead forms … to the permanent principles of good architecture … in a constant desire to produce works of plastic art in the purest sense of expression." His passion about plastic lyricism was evident to his new friends, and the thesis also clarified one of the unique characteristics of Brazilian modernism.

Vernacular lattice screen, Egypt
Creative Commons Wikimedia

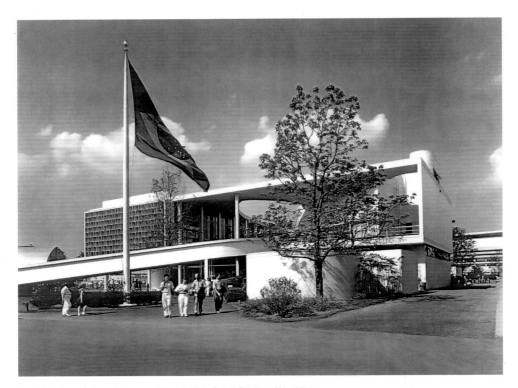

Lucio Costa and Oscar Niemeyer, World's Fair, Brazil Pavilion, New York
Creative Commons Wikimedia

Forever the teacher, Cret intervened at this point, explaining to Lucio and reminding Tingbo of a point he had made in a lantern slide lecture he'd given at the Philadelphia T-Square Club: blind allegiance to the newest techniques, and the corresponding neglect of regional variation yields sad results: "The tendency to unification, even in the Far East," he said, "[brings] unification of architectural vocabulary. [That's] sad. For then, then the geographical location tends to lose its earlier importance as a factor determining character." Character, he'd learnt from the great French teacher and theorist Julien Guadet, is essential in architecture. "Greater independence [from] natural conditions does not make for personality." Our technological gain is sometimes our cultural loss.

Vernacular lattice screen wall and door, China
©David Leatherbarrow

Lucio Costa, Parque Guinle, São Paulo, detail of lattice screen
©David Leatherbarrow

Paul Philippe Cret, vernacular study
©University of Pennsylvania Libraries

Shifting himself from the verandah shadows into the light, Tingbo said that he enjoyed working on sloped sites, for inclined terrain called for solutions that required both architectural art and engineering. Lucio asked if he had an example he could explain. "More than a few," was the reply, the confidence of which didn't conceal a sense of accomplishment. He prefaced his description with the point that mountains and rivers in combination, *shān shuǐ*, have always been thought to offer the most favorable place for building in Chinese culture—also, of course, landscape painting. The case recently added to his portfolio was the Sun-Ke house in Chongqing, the city to which he himself had relocated because of the war. Not only was the slope decisive, so was the climate.

Hearing about the layout, Lucio said: "Tingbo you've made matters unnecessarily difficult for yourself with the circular plan." Tingbo didn't refer to the great circular houses in southern China in his defense; instead, he elaborated on the ways the form, in plan and section, allowed the building to moderate the climate, while reforming the location. Sites aren't given to architects, they must be constructed, as architecture. Outside air is admitted at the newly terraced base, then channeled vertically, through stack effect, to increase both air flow and cooling. Improbable as the form may have seemed, the solution, he maintained, is no less intelligent than the countless mountainside buildings in China's long architectural history. But air, it seems, was not all that flowed in his architecture. Likewise, people. This would be particularly evident years later in the other house he would build for Sun-Ke, in Nanjing, where people *flowed* from room to room, thanks to implied diagonals within an aggregate of volumes whose corners had been removed, in the manner of Wright, whom he would meet on another visit to the US.

Yang Tingbo, Sun Ke's home "The Round House," Chongqing, 1940

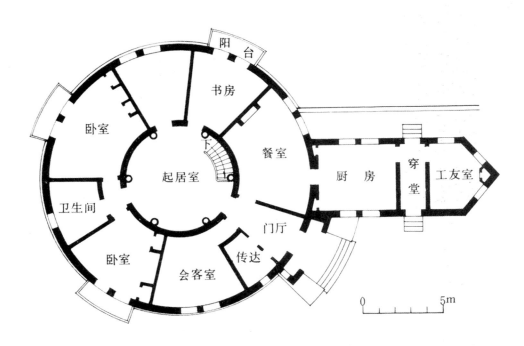

Yang Tingbo, Sun Ke House, Chongqing, plan
Nanjing Institute of Technology, Institute of Architecture, *Yang Tingbao Architectural Design Collection*
(Beijing: China Architecture and Building Press), 1983, 116.

Traditional circular houses *(tulou)*, Chuxi, Fujian Province, China
©David Leatherbarrow

Yang Tingbo, Sun Ke House, Nanjing, 2012
Creative Commons Wikimedia

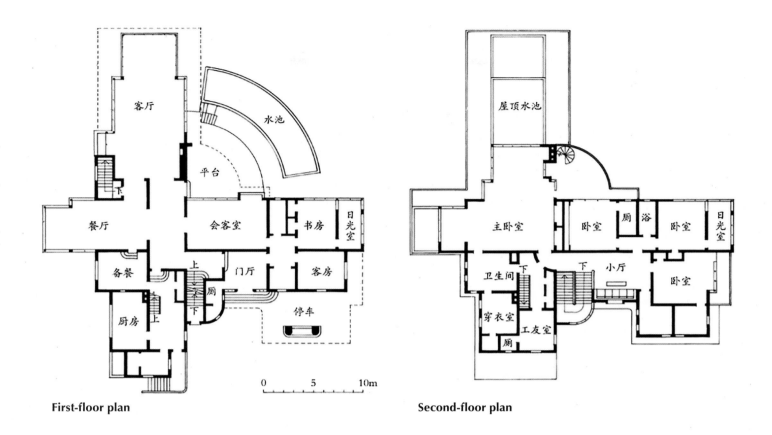

First-floor plan

客厅　水池　平台　餐厅　会客室　书房　日光室　备餐　上　下　门厅　客房　厨房　上　下　厕　停车

0　5　10m

Second-floor plan

屋顶水池　主卧室　卧室　厕　浴　卧室　日光室　卫生间　下　下　小厅　卧室　穿衣室　工友室　厕

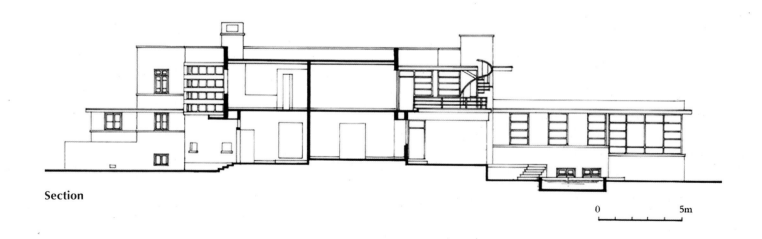

Section

0　5m

Yang Tingbo, Sun Ke House, Nanjing, plans redrawn by Li Zhitao
Li Zhitao, Bao Li, Wu Jinxiu, eds., *The Complete Works of Yang Tingbo, vol. 1*
(Beijing: China Architecture and Building Press, 2021), 417.

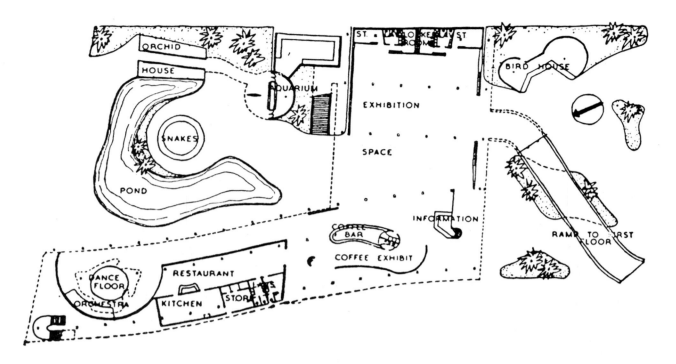

Costa and Niemeyer, Brazil Pavilion
©Lucio Costa Registro de Uma Vivência

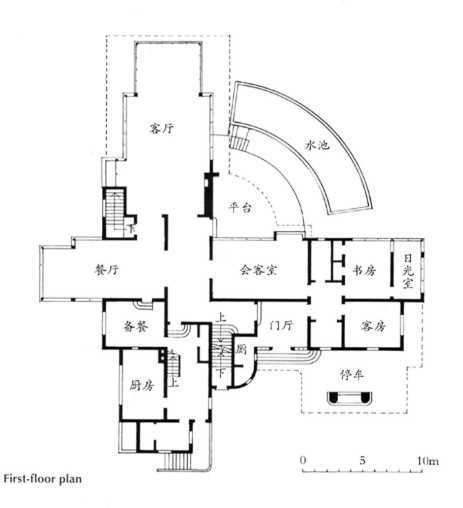

First-floor plan

Sun Ke House, Nanjing, plans redrawn by Li Zhitao
Li Zhitao, Bao Li, Wu Jinxiu, eds., *The Complete Works of Yang Tingbo, vol. 1*
(Beijing: China Architecture and Building Press, 2021), 417.

Also decisive is the rather beautifully modulated section. Of course, that project didn't enter into the veranda conversation any more than Lucio's Parque Guinle or Cret's burial in the nearby cemetery; but what was then Tingbo's future project does indicate, to anyone who reads the transcript of the verandah conversation, his commitment to modern conditions of both the environment and culture. On this point, he found himself in perfect agreement with Lucio, for whom graceful movement through variously opened and enclosed volumes was a primary intention, particularly in the Brazil Pavilion. Lucio explained that the curve of the Pavilion site "was an aspect that presided over the entire layout of the project. It was the central motif … the fracture of rigidity, this ordered movement running from one side of the composition indeed holds a baroque quality—in the positive sense of the word."

As the discussion moved toward its end, Cret said he rather liked their surprisingly common understandings of the types of problems modernity and modernization presented architects in places as diverse as Brazil, China, and the United States, the solutions of which attested as much to environmental and cultural differences as to the fundamental task of modern architecture. But just as he started to explain what he was working on at the nearby Penn campus, a new building for the chemistry faculty, the hybridity of which showed as much struggle as success, Madame Cret appeared on the verandah and said that because the sun was passing behind the cemetery trees and trolley traffic was increasing with the end of the workday, it might be a good time to come into the house for a glass of wine or cup of tea. She added that maybe on some future occasion they could return to their questions concerning modern and contemporary architecture in Brazil and China—suggesting, it seems, in these countries modernity would remain an ongoing project.

A Map, a Conversation, and a Bridge

Louise Noelle Gras
Professor, Universidad Nacional Autónoma de México

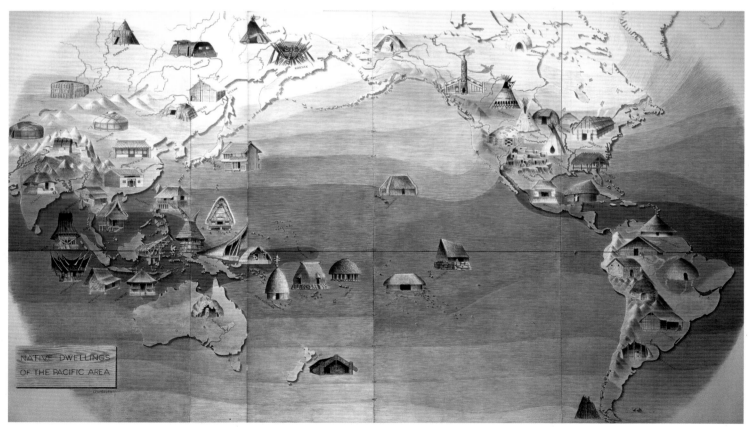

Miguel Covarrubias, *Native dwellings of the Pacific area*, 1939; originally painted for the Golden Gate International Exhibition, and located in the Pacific House
Miguel Covarrubias en México y en San Francisco, Mexico, INAH, 2007, p. 12

In 1939, the painter and ethnographer Miguel Covarrubias, executed six large panels in the Pacific House, one of the main halls of the Golden Gate International Exposition, in Treasure Island, San Francisco, California.[1] Yes, it was the same year that the imaginary "Verandah conversation" took place, presented by Professor David Leatherbarrow as part of the first session of the China–Brazil Architecture Forum. He stated that the exchange was about modernism, architectural practice, history, geography and, of course, culture. It is a fictional conversation that I particularly enjoyed, with the reminiscence of Paul Philippe Cret, Lucio Costa, and Yang Tingbao, that will lead me to other considerations.

For the moment, I would like to concentrate on the Golden Gate exhibition, and the idea that a bridge, a magnificent one, was the start of the project.[2] I would be keen to think of the five sessions of the China–Brazil Architecture Forum as monumental bridges, traversing land and oceans, to join thoughts and knowledge through the immaterial wonders of the internet. Connections that materialized during the presentations, particularly with the Jishou Art Museum and Bridge by Yung Ho Chang/Atelier FCJZ.

The November Saturday/Sunday meetings of architects and scholars, through the wonders of the new media possibilities, was appreciated by me from Mexico as a kind of central milestone, the same way as Miguel Covarrubias intended eighty years ago. Indeed, in the Pacific House and under the protection of a Mayan deity, the people related to the vast ocean came together in another fruitful conversation. The site consisted of a large hall, embracing knowledge, languages, crafts, and cordiality, inviting the visitors to admire distant cultures. Covarrubias was a Mexican artist who had traveled extensively through the rim of the Pacific Ocean, with the eyes of a researcher and an ethnographer, that allowed him to achieve the exceptional panels of the *Pacific Pageant*.[3] One of these panels, *Peoples of the Pacific*, permits me to talk about the different persons, related in many ways, that inhabited the web for the past five weeks.

I will start with the friends who devised the idea of the China–Brazil Architecture Forum "Modernity as an Ongoing Project": Li Xiangning, from the College of Architecture and Urban Planning, Tongji University; and Carlos Eduardo Comas, from the Committee of Architectural Criticism-ASC, PROPAR of the Faculdade

de Arquitetura, Universidade Federal do Rio Grande do Sul. They were accompanied in the opening session by David Leatherbarrow, as part of this original venture. It is important to acknowledge that this project could not be held in person, due to COVID-19 restrictions: we all met via the internet. I have been lucky enough to travel to China where I had the privilege of meeting with Wang Shu and Lu Wenyu, in the China University of Art, and of enjoying the Huang Gongwang Museum in Fuyan. On the other hand, I have visited Brazil several times, having the opportunity to encounter Paulo Mendez da Rocha in his São Paulo apartment ten years ago. Both circumstances are sources of pride, stressing my good fortune.

Li Xiangning, Wang Shu, and Yung Ho Chang, Qu Zhou, China, 2018
©Gao Changjun

Carlos Comas, Fernando Diez, and David Leatherbarrow, Maceió, Brazil, 2012
©Louise Noelle Gras

Lu Wenyu, Carlos Comas, and Louise Noelle Gras at the Huang Gongwang Museum, Fuyan, China, 2016
Photograph from Louise Noelle Gras' archive

Paolo Mendes da Rocha and Louise Noelle Gras, São Paulo, Brazil, 2011
©Louise Noelle Gras

Luis Barragán, Casa Prieto López, Mexico City, 1952
©Louise Noelle Gras

In the case of the new conversations that took place during November 2021, I thought that an adequate site was needed and I went on reviewing the suitable architectural real estate. Close to my home, I found an ample living room provided by Luis Barragán, in the Prieto López House,[4] and closer to Carlos Comas, I discovered a great installation in Brumaldinho, Minas Gerais,[5] that brought about the remembrance of Tarsila do Amaral, introduced by Renato Anelli in his presentation. On the other side of the ocean, closer to all the Chinese friends, I thought that a wonderful dialogue could be held in the Reception Center for Faculty and Visiting Professors of the China Art Academy, in Hangzhou, by Amateur Architecture Studio. It probably embodies the perfect verandah. Other options could have been Laurent Troost´s Casa Campirana, in Manaus, or Zhu Pei´s Imperial Kiln Museum, in Jingdezhen. What a delight to meet on those terraces with the organizers and all the presenters.

Amateur Architecture Studio, China Art Academy, Reception Center for Faculty and Visiting Professors, Hangzhou, China, 2002–2007
©Leonardo Finotti

Laurent Troost, Casa Campirana, Manaus, Brazil, 2017
©Leonardo Finotti

Zhu Pei Studio, Imperial Kiln Museum, Jingdezhen, China, 2020
Photograph supplied by Zhu Pei Studio

Referring to the opening talk, it is relevant to establish that, on one hand, Carlos Comas had written a lucid analysis of Brazilian modernity and all its complexity, "The Poetics of Development: Notes on two Brazilian Schools";[6] on the other hand Li Xiangning, published ten years ago in *AV* an enlightening article,[7] providing us with the insight of the key concepts of Chinese architecture. Their knowledge and analysis were quite illuminating for the Forum, apparent in their thoughtful approaches to the themes. Also, in the second talk, there were the theoretical dissertations of professors Renato Anelli and, especially, Pei Zhao, who explained the early interest of Chinese architects in Brazilian architecture, after the 1963 UIA Congress in Cuba.

For the rest, the attendants were immersed in the ongoing architectural modernity as a project, with appealing presentations.

Facing the diversity of places and themes, one of the main concerns was to try to find communicating vessels or conductive lines through the varied and rich array of works presented by fourteen leading architects of China and Brazil. Perhaps the principal ideas could be in architectural genres, or in ways of building, materials, and functions, or the response to climate and nature, or to urban environment. Here are some of my thoughts about the four sessions.

I considered that museums were present in almost all the lectures. Of course, this leads me to contemplate further how museums seem to be the temples of modernity, attracting many visitors interested in the buildings as much as in their collections.

Naturally, the presentations started with Amateur Architecture Studio, with Wang Shu

and Lu Wenyu, and the Historic Museum, in Ningbo, China (2008). The respect for the site and for tradition was laid as the foundation for a cultural compound that encompasses the museum and other facilities. The construction used a traditional technique, called *wapan*, reusing varied materials to create a solid appealing structure.

Zhu Pei in his studio, designed the Imperial Kiln Museum, Jingdezhen, China (2020). The complex consists of nine oblong buildings surrounding the archaeological site of the original Ming Dinasty Porcelain Kiln. Each structure has a particular purpose, achieving unity through the use of vaulted structures, recovered with recycled bricks.

Andrade-Morettin Architects, Moreira Salles Institute, São Paulo, Brazil, 2017
©Leonardo Finotti

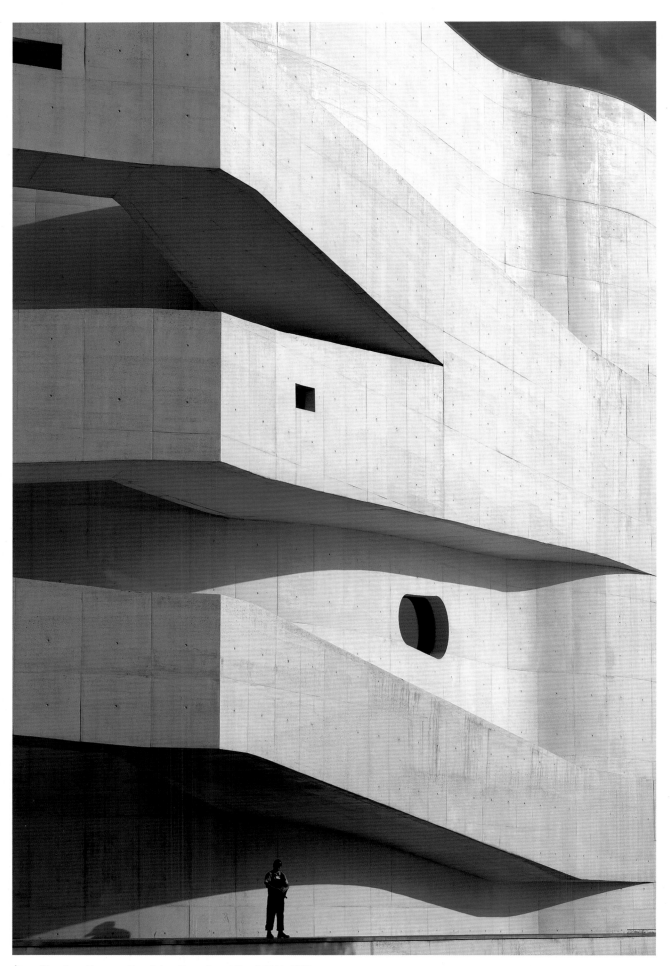

Álvaro Siza, Ibere Camargo Foundation, Porto Alegre, Brazil, 2003–2007
©Leonardo Finotti

Andrade-Morettin Architects, represented by Vinicius Andrade, showed the urban Moreira Salles Institute, in São Paulo, Brazil, completed in 2017. Located in a small lot on Avenida Paulista, the vertical museum, archive, and institute offer a public plaza in the third level, and natural ventilation in the circulation spaces. The construction was a *tour de force*, due to the small size of the terrain, that the architects were able to achieve with engineer José Luiz Canal.

José Luiz Canal as project manager, was in charge of the design of Álvaro Siza, for the Ibere Camargo Foundation, Porto Alegre, Brazil (2003–2007). A complicated structure, mainly because of the floating closed bridges that form the main facade, was achieved by the skill and dedication of the engineer.

Martin Corullon, with Corullon & Cedroni, has been working on an expansion of the Museum of Art São Paulo, MASP, in Brazil, which will open in 2024. It consists of a slender, sober, and tall building, due to the small lot, and will maintain the preponderance of the original museum by Lina Bo Bardi. They started by refurbishing the initial building and recuperating the innovative interior design.

As mentioned before, Yung Ho Chang/Atelier FCJZ designed the Jishou Art Museum and Bridge, China (2019), revisiting the tradition of covered bridges in that mountainous area. This condition allowed the designer to locate a museum above the passageway, avoiding the idea of a freestanding building far from the central part of the town.

The proposal of a museum that integrates a new structure into an old building was adopted by Marcelo Ferraz y Francisco Fanucci, for the Ilopolis Bread Museum, Brazil (2005–2008). The structure of a centenary wheat mill is at the center of the complex, which includes exhibition halls, a teaching kitchen, and a cafeteria.

Liu Yichun of Atelier Deshaus, had a similar proposal for the Long Museum, West Bund, Shanghai, China (2011–2014), conserving part of the coal unloading system that was distributed through the adjacent Huangpu River. The new building adopts the exposed concrete, using a cantilever structure for a vault-umbrella-like ceiling. A sober white box encloses ample showrooms, where large windows and skylights allow for generous natural light.

These last projects directed me to observe that the recuperation or reuse was a significant part of the thoughts and the projects of several architects, whether they refurbished a building or tried to recover simple ruins. It is not only the proposal of conserving a monument, but a trend that the twenty-first century has brought about, as part of the effort to minimize our carbon imprint, with various approaches worth examining.

In Brazil, as it was signaled, Marcelo Ferraz and Francisco Fanucci carried out an accurate recuperation at the Ilopolis Bread Museum, leading to the improvement of a small village. Likewise, Martin Corullon and Gustavo Cedroni cared for the restoration of Lina Bo Bardi´s MASP, restructuring the building and the recuperating of the daring exhibit proposal. Marta Moreira, MMBB, presented a work done in collaboration with Paulo Mendes da Rocha: the SESC Plaza de Mayo, São Paulo, Brazil (2017), consisting of a complex array of recreational facilities and services in an existing building. The exemplary transformation conveys the recovery of activities in a central area of the city.

Atelier FCJZ, Jishou Art Museum and Bridge, China, 2019
Photograph supplied by Atelier FCJZ

Liu Yichun, Atelier Deshaus, Long Museum, West Bund, Shanghai, China, 2011–2014
©Louise Noelle Gras

In Shanghai, Liu Yichun, Atelier Deshaus, not only moved toward the conservation at the Long Museum, but worked on the silos renovation in the eastern part of the city. Here exterior escalators enhance the view toward the Huangpu River, and the silos are partially occupied by a museum, to achieve the "Poetic de-composition of architecture," suggested by the architect.

These considerations linked with other themes that recurrently occupied the illuminating lectures, such as the concern with materials and their use, as was pointed out by Wang Shu and Lu Wenyu in their presentation of the Historic Museum in Ningbo. Also, Zhu Pei was keen in reusing bricks at the Imperial Kiln Museum, and Zhang Lei was interested in "brick and stone," apparent in the two brick houses for a poet in a small village in Nanjing (2007), and the stone Lei House in Hangzhou (2017), both in China. However, in Brazil, the main considerations included the search of a pleasing relationship between industrial materials, like steel with exposed concrete

for the tall São Paulo buildings of Andrade-Morettin Architects and Marta Moreira with Paulo Mendes da Rocha.

Landscape design was not especially addressed by Chinese architects, despite the long-standing tradition of the Chinese garden, as exemplified by the Humble Administrator´s Garden in Suzhou, near Shanghai. On the other hand, Brazil offered varied examples, following the twentieth dazzling example of Roberto Burle Marx, taking advantage of a tropical vegetation that allows for a luscious environment.

Some architects, like Laurent Troost showed a major interest in the adequate use of vegetation, as in the award-winning Casa Campirana (2017), and Casa Guaporé (2019), both in Manaus, Brazil. A special wager was the Casarao de Inovacao Cassina (2020), refurbishing a centenary hotel in ruins and conquered by vegetation, at the center of the same Amazonian city. The site offers several spaces to foster creativity, conserving at the same time the old facade with a layer of vegetation.

Paulo Mendes da Rocha and Marta Moreira, MMBB, SESC Plaza de Mayo, São Paulo, Brazil, 2017
©Leonardo Finotti

Laurent Troost, Casina, Manaus, Brazil, 2020
©Joana França

In downtown São Paulo, Angelo Bucci, SPBR Arquitetos, built a weekend house (2013), with and innovative and challenging program, taking advantage of the generosity of the local flora. It is noteworthy to see the choice to locate the pool and solarium on the upper floor, with facilities for the owners and visitors in the lower levels, surrounded by a well-chosen variety of plants.

In China an important attempt was made by Cui Kai in the Garden Expo Park in a suburb of Nanjing, China, in 2021. The site had ten tall silos, witness of a sustained exploitation of the mountain for a cement plant, but the verdant foggy setting allowed a new vocation: a cultural and commercial complex.

Other concepts can be raised from the presentations, rich in ideas and visual materials, that allow the opportunity to appreciate far away architectural works. The China–Brazil Architecture Forum allowed the attendants to discover the ideas of the architects, to compare and consider them. The five sessions brought important lessons, especially for someone like me, fortunate to have visited these two amazing countries that keep changing, surprising us with their ongoing modernity projects, the wealth and creativity of their architects and their enduring culture. It will be important to meet again to broaden our awareness, to be able to fill new contemporary maps with buildings and people, and to have more conversations with the construction of many golden bridges. We will all be richer for that.

Angelo Bucci, Weekend House, São Paulo, Brazil, 2013
©Nelson Khon

Land-based Rationalism DRC, Garden Expo Park, Nanjing, China, 2021
Photograph supplied by Land-based Rationalism DRC

Golden Gate Bridge, San Francisco, United States, 2012
©Ricardo Alvarado

[1] *Miguel Covarrubias en México y en San Francisco* (Mexico: INAH, 2007). The assistant of Covarrubias was the painter, Antonio Ruiz.

[2] The Golden Gate International Exposition was held in 1939 and 1940 to celebrate the opening of San Francisco–Oakland Bay Bridge in 1936 and the Golden Gate Bridge in 1937.

[3] To know more about Miguel Covarrubias see "Los territorios artísticos de Miguel Covarrubias," Rita Eder (ed.), *Anales Del Instituto De Investigaciones Estéticas*, Suplemento (Mexico: UNAM, 2020).

[4] "Luis Barragán's House in Pedregal. A Successful Restauration," *Docomomo Journal*, no. 52, Lisboa, 2015.

[5] Cildo Merieles, *Inmensa*, (Minas Gerais, Brazil: Brumaldinho, 2002).

[6] Carlos Eduardo Comas, "The Poetics of Development: Notes on Two Brazilian Schools," *Latin America in Construction. Architecture 1955–1980* (New York: MoMA, 2015).

[7] Li Xiangning, "Key Concepts of Chinese Architecture Today," *AV*, no. 150, Madrid, 2011.

Figurative Structures: The Construction of Meaning in Brazilian Modern Architecture

Renato Anelli
Associate Professor, Mackenzie University

In those years, in the immediate postwar period, it was like a beacon of light shining in a death camp.

Lina Bo Bardi, 1990

Interior of the bedroom at Casa Modernista, by Gregori Warchavchik, São Paulo, 1930. Postcard painting, by Tarsila do Amaral, 1924; quilt by Regina Gomide Graz.
Photograph Hugo Zanella
Gregori Warchavchik, Photographic Collection

Poetically comparing her memories of the first images she had seen of Brazilian modern architecture with a "beacon of light," Lina Bo Bardi, an Italian architect who immigrated to Brazil in 1946, bears witness to the strong impact of the publication of *Brazil Builds: Architecture New and Old, 1652–1942*, in 1943. The catalog of the exhibition held at the Museum of Modern Art (MoMA) in New York presented a wide range of works, revealing its extensive production distributed throughout the country, which included the main projects by Oscar Niemeyer built up to that time. Brazilian modern architecture stood out on the international scene for developing a peculiar aesthetic associated with the rapid growth of Brazilian cities.

By carrying on a posture originated in the 1920s, the new architecture intended to be modern and Brazilian. It brought about a notion developed by Mário de Andrade, an intellectual, poet, and activist of the pioneering Semana de Arte Moderna (Modern Art Week) who had a strong role in the cultural construction of Brazil's modernization in the 1930s. When commenting on the internationalism of the first abstract modern houses built in São Paulo, Andrade believed it to be a transient characteristic, which would be overcome by "the search for and fixation of elements of Brazilian architectural constancy," concluding, "It is through them that, within modern architecture, Brazil will make the contribution it is due to make."[1]

With this objective in mind, the first modern architects sought something that could define Brazil as their works' origin, allowing them to be internationally recognized as Brazilian. Interestingly, the first architect to design and build a successful work in this line was the Ukrainian Gregori Warchavchik in 1927. Trained in Rome in 1921, Warchavchik immigrated to Brazil in 1923, settling in São Paulo. He lived among modernist intellectuals and worked at Companhia Construtora de Santos, a company that introduced important productive modernizations in construction.

In 1927 he built his own house with shapes that could fit both Italian rationalism and the geometric abstractionism of central European architecture. However, the garden designed by his wife, Mina Klabin, used plants from the native flora, many of them represented in the painting by the modernist Tarsila do Amaral, hanging on the wall of his modernist house built in 1930. The first modern architecture used native flora and landscaping, inspired by the modernist plastic arts in order to acclimatize its international abstractionism to Brazil.

Vista da Ilha de Itamaracá, Frans Post, 1637
©Royal Picture Gallery Mauritshuis, The Hague

Territory, Colony, Young Nation:
The Construction of Cultural Identity

We highlight the modernist painter Tarsila do Amaral, a student of Fernand Lèger in Paris (1923). Her drawings and paintings interpret the landscape, the vegetation, and the man that the colonizers met when they occupied the territory that would become Brazil.

In contrast to countries like China, which originated in a millenary empire, Brazil stems from the Portuguese colonization of a territory originally occupied by Indigenous peoples. This condition is well described by Indigenous leader Ailton Krenak:

_____

Here in this region of the world, which the most recent memory decided to call America, in its more restricted part, which we call Brazil, long before it was "America" and long before having a border stamp that separates neighboring and distant countries, our great families already lived here. These great families of ours, who already lived here, are those who are recognized as tribes today.[2]

_____

The Portuguese conquest of this territory started in 1500, embroiled in a dispute with other European countries, such as Spain, France, and Holland. Portugal created an empire on the American and African coasts of the South Atlantic, extending it toward Asia, across the Indian and Pacific Oceans, establishing trading posts in India, China, and Japan.

Some of the most notorious paintings recording Brazil's landscape, nature, and inhabitants date from the occupation of part of its colonial territory by the Dutch (1630–1654). The art historian Margareth Pereira[3] identifies in the paintings by Frans Post and Albert Eckhout the emergence of a new sensitivity toward nature, which should be tamed so that the civilization effort would not be crushed.

Such sensitivity was displayed by two Swiss-French men in their visits to Brazil, in the 1920s, at the invitation of the modernists.

Urbanisme, Rio de Janeiro, Brazil, Le Corbusier, 1929
©FLC/ADAGP

In 1924, the writer Blaise Cendrars came to São Paulo and from there he set out to tour the interior of the country. The excursion to the old colonial cities of the eighteenth century is worthy of note, where he visited the baroque churches and palaces set between hills. He was accompanied by Oswald de Andrade, Mário de Andrade, and Tarsila do Amaral, who recorded the trip in drawings he later published. That was the first modernist interpretation of such architecture, emphasizing the relationship between the buildings of that period and the natural landscape.

The second French-Swiss visitor was the architect Le Corbusier, who in 1929 came to São Paulo and Rio de Janeiro from Buenos Aires and Montevideo. In each of the four cities, he conceived megastructures that interact with the landscape and presented them in the form of sketches at conferences. Those were not real projects, but the formulation of a concept.

Le Corbusier considered it possible to repeat the grandeur of Greek and Roman monuments in the intensity of their presence in the landscape.

———

When we are in Rio de Janeiro—the lapis lazuli bays, sky and water, succeed each other in the distance in the form of an arch, decorated with white piers and pink beaches … as everything is then party and spectacle, everything is joy inside us, everything contracts itself to keep the flourishing idea … we are possessed by a violent, maybe insane, desire to essay, here too, a human adventure—the desire to play a man-affirmation game against or along with the presence-nature. [4]

———

This "man-affirmation game" was an important motto for the development of the most intense projects of Brazilian modern architecture in the following years.

We can identify two lines of development.

One is the relationship between elongated horizontal forms, such as Le Corbusier's megastructure, and the profile of the landscape, the great mountains in Rio de Janeiro—a concept applied by Affonso Eduardo Reidy in the Pedregulho housing project. The other is the reproduction of this natural profile in the built volumes essentially defined by the structure itself, which can be identified in the work of Oscar Niemeyer starting with Pampulha.

Let's get back to the first one. Le Corbusier made his sketches of megastructures to present at conferences. He defined the scales of the

Residential viaduct, detail of Rio de Janeiro megastructure, Le Corbusier 1936. Model by Yannis Tsiomis in his book *Le Corbusier: Rio de Janeiro*, 1929–1936
©FLC/ADAGP

structure that meanders between the hills and the coastal plains. The simulation of this structure in a model and photomontages made by Yannis Tsiomis in his book *Le Corbusier: Rio de Janeiro, 1929–1936*[5] show a city still predominantly horizontal, on its way to verticalization. Aiming at concentrating the diffuse verticalization process in this megastructure, detached from the ground by large columns, would allow for the continuity of the horizontality of the plains without volumetric interruption.

Although the proposal had not even been considered by the municipality, the message was heard by many architects. The 1936 visit coincided with the acceleration of the social-housing public policy initiated by Getúlio Vargas' government after the 1930 national revolution. Among the large modern housing projects developed in the following decades, it was Affonso Reidy's in Pedregulhos, Rio de

Janeiro, that received the greatest recognition for its architectural quality. Promoted by the Department of Popular Housing of the Federal District (1944–1948), it constituted a fragment of what could have been a modern large-scale urbanization plan.

The best example of this poetic procedure is Oscar Niemeyer's projects in Pampulha. It can be observed in the profile of the reinforced concrete vaults of the Church of São Francisco de Assis, which reproduce the mountains and plants profiles, painted by Tarsila do Amaral in Postcard, in the section of the structure. The winding Casa do Baile's marquee, following the edges of the island where it is located, follows the same planning procedure. Neither baroque nor expressionist, there is similarity between the structural profiles and the figurative form intended to express a poetics of economy of means, whose equivalence is attributed to the paintings of Henri Matisse and Hans Arp.[6]

If, at the scale of the building, this relation of figurative representation of the landscape in the structural form was quickly built, the urban dimension of the Corbusian game found greater difficulties in becoming effective.

Visiting Brazil again in 1936 to collaborate with Lucio Costa on the project for the Ministry of Education and Public Health's building, Le Corbusier had to face the master plan block model developed by French urban planner Alfred Agache a few years earlier. For the Castelo region, where the construction was meant to be built, the plan stipulated that the buildings should be aligned along the perimeter of the blocks, with no frontal setback, and maintain the unity of facades and contour plan. Le Corbusier tried to avoid those limitations by looking for another piece of land on Avenida Beira Mar, where he could establish a direct relationship with the sea, the beach, and the hills.

Pedregulho Housing Estate, Aphonso Eduardo Reidy, Rio de Janeiro, 1944–1948
©Leonardo Finotti

Oscar Niemeyer, Church of São Francisco de Assis, Pampulha, 1942–1944
©Leonardo Finotti

Oscar Niemeyer, Ball House, Pampulha, Belo Horizonte, 1942–1944
©Leonardo Finotti

Upon his return to Paris, he received the confirmation denying the change of places proposed by him, and so the team led by Lucio Costa assumed the new project on the original lot.

The project did not follow the guidelines of the Agache Plan, opting to redefine Le Corbuseir's proposal: from the long horizontal building supported by 4-meter columns by the sea, to a vertical building with a blade-shaped volume supported by 10-meter columns, and crossed transversally by a low volume arranged on one of the sides of the block. Thus, it created a public square under the building, opening a void amid the dense urban volume of closed blocks specified by the plan for the region. An urbanistic conception of modern architecture was inaugurated there, which complemented a process of urban modernization without being guided by the precepts disseminated by the Congrès Internationaux d'Architecture Moderne (CIAM). Originated in Rio de Janeiro, this concept found its best expression in São Paulo.

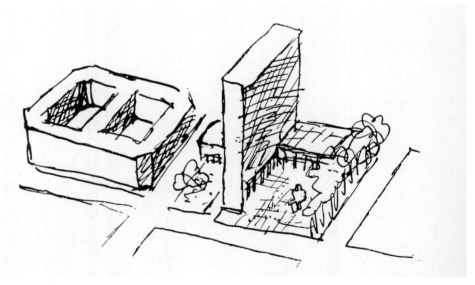

Le Corbusier, sketch of Ministry of Education and Public Health, Oeuvre Complete, 1938–1946
©FLC/ADAGP

The Rapid Urbanization of Brazilian Cities and Its Implications for Architecture: Modern Architecture in Dense Urban Fabric

Then the capital of Brazil, Rio de Janeiro entered the twentieth century with 811,000 inhabitants, reaching 1.15 million in 1920, and 2.37 million in 1950. Center of the nineteenth-century agricultural coffee economy and twentieth-century industrialization, São Paulo grew faster. The population of 239,000 inhabitants in 1900 reached 1.32 million in 1940, surpassing that of Rio de Janeiro in 1950, when it reached 2.19 million. The urban model of this demographic growth was cities that verticalized their urban centers, using the most advanced technology of reinforced concrete, and spread out precariously on the periphery. The Brazilian vanguards of modern architecture acted in this process of urban modernization, but never dominated it to the point of imposing their urban principles. The modern urbanism of Brasília is, therefore, an exception in a country that carried on its urban planning according to North American and French guidelines. From the 1930s onwards, the modern orientation became more present in the construction of public buildings, such as social housing, schools, hospitals, and even in the construction of private apartment and office buildings.

However, this presence was never the most preponderant in urban transformation, except in the pages of architecture publications.

It is important to note that the main formal poetics of modern Brazilian architecture was developed in the initial phase of the growth of cities, focusing more on the relationship with tropical nature than urban challenges. The comparison between two projects by Oscar Niemeyer carried out in the early 1950s can help us understand the problem.

Casa das Canoas, the architect's residence designed in 1951 in a diffuse urbanization region to the south of the city of Rio de Janeiro, is presented in such a way as to emphasize the reverberation between the sinuous forms of its roof slab with the mountains that surround it, covered by dense vegetation.

That same year, the architect designed a set of apartment buildings in the central region of São Paulo, among which the Copan building stands out. Niemeyer faced the challenge of verticalization in density, housing about five thousand residents in 1,160 apartments spread over 32 floors. The winding building refers to Le Corbusier's megastructure, despite presenting relevant differences: in addition to the absence of the road system on the roof, the building is inserted in an urban lot and is not "detached from the ground" by columns. On the contrary, the city floor organizes the first two floors, which offer shops and services in continuity with the surrounding urban fabric.

In São Paulo, density imposed itself, verticalizing a land structure that was formed between the nineteenth and twentieth centuries, transformed by the Prestes Maia's Avenues Plan from 1930. It takes time for a modern architecture like that of the Ministry of Education's building to emerge in São Paulo, which is at the same time both an architectural and urban act of opening up free space for public use. Housing projects, public schools, and university campuses are experiences that mark the horizontal expansion of the city from the 1940s onwards.

Reinforced Concrete Structures Making Room for a New Monumentality

Designed by Lina Bo Bardi in 1957 and inaugurated only in 1968, the Museum of Art of São Paulo (MASP) is the first and most striking realization of an open space defined by the building's configuration. Projecting itself on the main ridge of the city, where Paulista Avenue is located, the museum was placed in a focal point of the Saracura stream valley, transformed into an avenue during the 1940s.

Lina Bo Bardi conceived a building divided into two volumes separated by a span of 74 meters. Through this gap, the ground level of the avenue at the ridge extends over the lower volume, accommodated on the slope, and under the volume raised by a powerful pre-stressed reinforced concrete structure. Thus, a public square is formed, open to the city, overlooking the valley, and whose use

by the population in political and cultural manifestations makes it one of the main symbolic spaces of the city of São Paulo.

Two decades later, Paulo Mendes da Rocha would use two projects to re-interpret the spatial arrangement created by Lina at MASP.

Lina Bo Bardi, Museum of Art of São Paulo (MASP), São Paulo, 1857–1968
©Nelson Kon

Paulo Mendes da Rocha, sketch of Brazilian Sculpture and Environment Museum, 1988
©Casa Da Arquitectura Collection

In 1988, the Brazilian Sculpture and Environment Museum (MUBE) created a plan that extends from the ridge level of Avenida Europa over the gently sloping terrain toward the Verde stream. The project creates a sequence of levels that accommodates an open-air auditorium and several terraces leading to the entrance to the underground museum. A pre-stressed reinforced concrete marquee creates a free span of 90 meters, which serves as a horizontal reference for the new ground where the sculptures are placed. The pioneering interpretation by Sophia Telles in 1990 suggests that this design action by Mendes da Rocha refers to the vast horizons of the natural landscape that has challenged Brazilian modern architecture since the conferences by Le Corbusier.[7] In the midst of a dense and vertical city, the marquee would be a possible horizon.

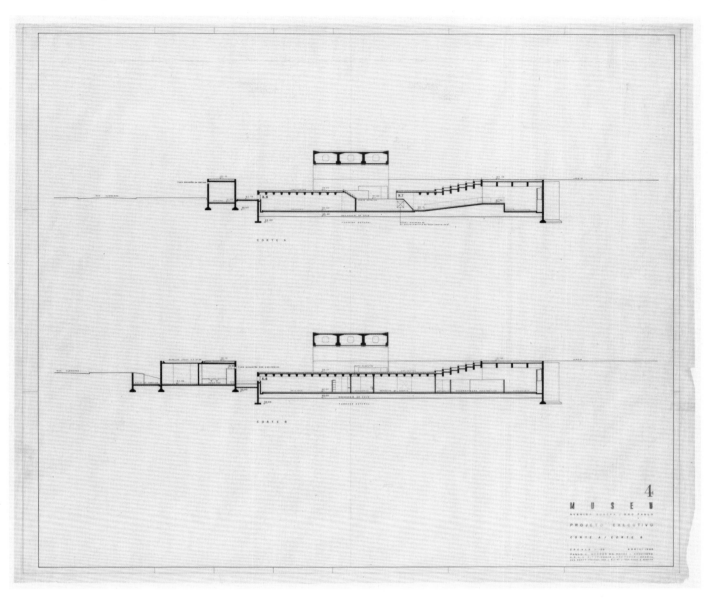

Paulo Mendes da Rocha, structural sections of the Brazilian Sculpture and Environment Museum, 1988
©Casa Da Arquitectura Collection

Paulo Mendes da Rocha, Brazilian Sculpture and Environment Museum, São Paulo, 1988
©Nelson Kon

Paulo Mendes da Rocha, Patriarca Square's view from the old colonial downtown, São Paulo, 1988
©Nelson Kon

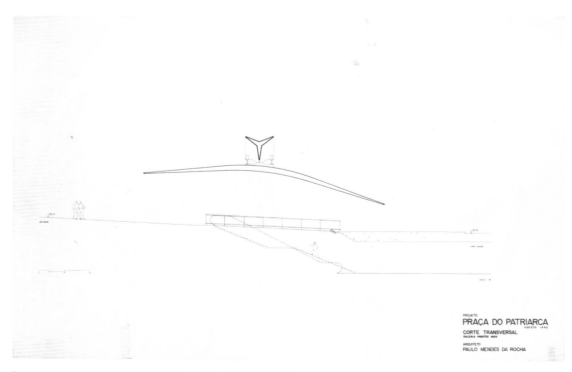

Paulo Mendes da Rocha, Patriarca Square section, São Paulo, 1988
©Casa Da Arquitectura Collection

Paulo Mendes da Rocha, Patriarca Square's view from Anhangabaú Valley, São Paulo, 1988
©Nelson Kon

Shortly after, in 1992, Mendes da Rocha carried out the same action in remodeling Patriarca Square in the city center. It is a square located on the edge of the first implantation of São Paulo, known as the Triangle. The top of a triangular hill, defined by the valley of the Anhangabaú stream to the west and the floodplain of the Tamanduateí river to the east, used the steep slopes for military defense since its foundation in 1554. The square had been inaugurated in 1912, after the demolition of old colonial mansions, for the connection with the west expansion of the city through a viaduct. In the 1930s, a gallery building was constructed, with a new viaduct's head for its roof. In addition to the art galleries, escalators connected the square on the upper level to the avenue at the bottom of the valley, overcoming a gap of 22 meters.

Mendes da Rocha's project had as its object the remodeling of the square's floor and the creation of a new roof for the staircase. For this, the architect conceived a steel portico with 40 meters of free span, under which a slightly curved roof with a steel structure would be fixed. The roof is defined by the scale of the valley and the monumental buildings that line its sides. It is positioned along the symmetry axis of Viaduto do Chá, which is flanked by four large buildings. Two are on the east side, between the square and the valley: the Matarazzo Building (Marcelo Piacentini, 1937) and the Conde de Prates Building (Giancarlo Palanti, 1957). Two are on the west side, beyond the valley: the Municipal Theater (Ramos de Azevedo, 1911) and the Alexandre Mackenzie building (Preston & Curtis, 1929).

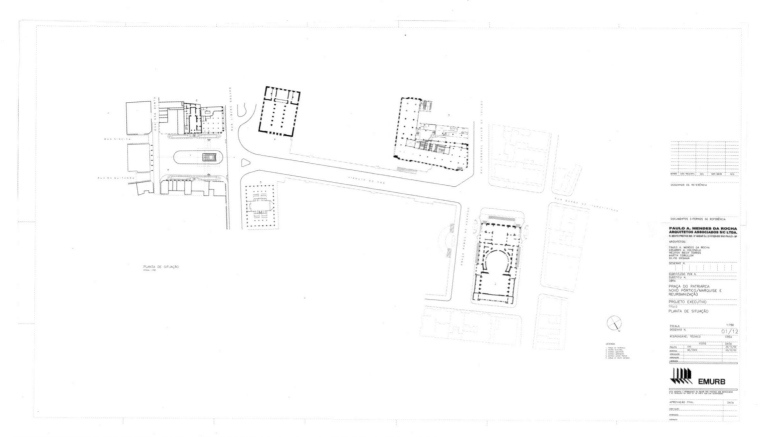

Patriarca Square's layout plan showing its position along the symmetry axis of Viaduto do Chá, which is flanked by four monumental buildings, represented by the ground-floor plans in the drawing
©Casa Da Arquitectura Collection

A curious layout plan, prepared for the publication of his work in 2000, represents the publicly accessible ground floors of these buildings, the viaduct floors, and the square with his intervention. Although it does not exactly follow the method of Nolli's map, which represented Rome through the contrast between full and empty spaces, it is possible to find the similarity in the representation of the portico areas and colonnaded balconies, which were part of the accessible voids. Mendes da Rocha selects from the urban fabric the elements he wants to complement, in this case the valley, the viaduct, and these four large buildings.

More recently, between 2006 and 2012, a team formed by Lina's former collaborator, Marcelo Ferraz, and the architects Chico Fanucci and

Marcos Cartum carried out the Praça das Artes project. Located a few meters away from the Municipal Theater, the complex serves as an annex for training musicians and dancers. The project is defined as a connection between Vale do Anhangabaú and the parallel street to the west, Rua Conselheiro Crispiniano, through the middle of the block. Occupying empty spaces and expanding them through the demolition of unusable buildings, it establishes an active dialogue with the existing urban space. Between preservations and new additions, the clear continuity of the open space drives the main decisions of the project.

The projects in São Paulo presented here marked a new line of modern intervention in dense vertical urban centers. The

controlled opening of free spaces through architectural intervention with a monumental character, even though the definition of this monumentality is the one presented by Lina when defending MASP's project:

> What I call monumental has nothing to do with size or "pomp" but relates to a sense of collectivity, that is, a collective consciousness. Anything that goes beyond the "particular," reaching out to the collective, can (and perhaps should) be monumental.[8]

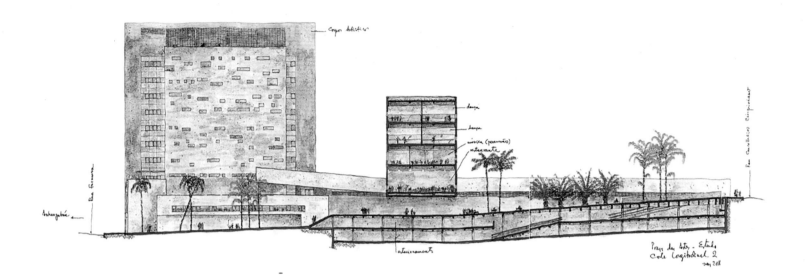

Brasil Arquitetura, Marcelo Ferraz, Chico Fanucci and Marcos Cartum, Arts Square, São Paulo, 2006

[1] Mário de Andrade, "Architectura Colonial III," *Diário Nacional, São Paulo*, (August 1928).

[2] Ailton Krenak, "Antes o mundo não existia" [The World Did Not Exist Before], *Tempo e história* (São Paulo: Cia das Letras, 1992).

[3] Margareth da Silva Pereira, "A arquitetura brasileira e o mito: Notas sobre um velho jogo entre afirmação-homem e presença natureza," *Gávea*, no. 8 (Rio de Janeiro. PUC-Rio. 1990), 2–21.

[4] Le Corbusier, *Precisões sobre um estado presente da arquitetura e do urbanismo* (São Paulo: Cosac & Naif, 2004), 227–229.

[5] Yannis Tsiomis, *Le Corbusier: Rio de Janeiro, 1929–1936* (Rio de Janeiro: Prefeitura do Rio de Janeiro, 1998).

[6] Sophia Telles, "Oscar Niemeyer: técnica e forma," *Óculum*, no. 2 (Campinas: PUC-Campinas, 1992), 4–7.

[7] Sophia Telles, *Museu da Escultura*, no. 32 (Oct/Nov 1990).

[8] Lina Bo Bardi, "O novo Trianon, 1957/67," *Mirante das Artes*, no. 5 (1967).

The Culture-driven Urban Regeneration in Shanghai

Jiang Jiawei
Assistant Professor, College of Architecture and Urban Planning, Tongji University

Since the 1990s, the city of Shanghai, a significant economic and population hub in China, has experienced a remarkable transformation in its downtown area. The policy of reform and opening up has accelerated the city's ability to attract foreign investment. Furthermore, the Chinese government, inspired by the success of the Guangdong experiment, has created a favorable environment for investment in Shanghai. The city's historical significance as the Pearl of the Orient from the 1910s to the 1930s has also left a lasting impression on the world, indirectly attracting more foreign capital to consider investing in this city as their entry into China. As a result, with the development of Pudong serving as a symbol of this transformative era, the early 1990s marked the beginning of both urban expansion and regeneration of the city center in Shanghai.

The renewal process of Shanghai's city center inevitably involves large-scale demolition and construction, a common occurrence in the renewal projects of many Chinese cities.

During this period, the urban expansion and redevelopment in Shanghai entailed demolishing deteriorated neighborhoods, relocating communities, and constructing modern towers. Unfortunately, this profit-driven development approach often prioritized convenience over preserving the city's urban fabric and historical identity. In 1996, the Municipal Government of Shanghai released a landmark document called *Several Opinions of Shanghai Municipality on Accelerating the Renovation of Dangerous Sheds and Shabby Houses of Central Parts of Shanghai.* This document played a crucial role in expediting urban renewal in Shanghai. Between 1991 and 1996, Shanghai demolished a total of 1.8 million square meters of hazardous sheds and dilapidated houses, combining land lease, real estate development, and municipal construction strategies. Notable renewal projects during this period included the development of the Xintiandi area by Shui On Land, and the Haihua Garden by the China Overseas Construction Company.

Prior to 2000, during a period of rapid urban construction in China, projects were primarily driven by capital without much consideration for their cultural impact. There was a lack of laws and regulations concerning preservation efforts. However, in the early-twenty-first century, Shanghai became the first Chinese city to gradually introduce the concept of "urban regeneration" as an alternative to "urban renewal." Other cities like Guangzhou and Shenzhen frequently employed the term "urban renewal for old city". In Guangzhou and Shenzhen, the focus on reconstructing old cities centered more on issues related to people's livelihoods, resulting in various public discussions. On the other hand, Shanghai's approach to urban regeneration turned to emphasize a culture-driven model, which became a distinct hallmark of the city's regeneration efforts. Following significant urban events, notably the 2010 Shanghai World Expo, Shanghai's urban regeneration model emerged as one of the leading examples of contemporary urban renovations in China.

Ateliers Jean Nouvel, Museum of Art Pudong
©Chen Hao

The Clustering Effect of Newly Emerging Cultural Architecture

Traditional cultural spaces in Shanghai are primarily found within the architectural heritage of the former concessions. These spaces include old-style museums, art galleries, and cultural palaces. During the early stages of urban renewal in Shanghai, these buildings were not immediately prioritized by the government and developers, since they were not perceived as directly addressing people's livelihood issues. As a result, the involvement of culture in urban renewal seemed unlikely.

However, after 2000, when the Shanghai regeneration project encompassed the redevelopment of industrial plots, large areas of land became available for continuous asset replacement. It thus created favorable conditions for the clustering effect, enabling the integration of traditional cultural spaces into urban regeneration. Shanghai began to establish a new mechanism of urban regeneration characterized by a culture-driven approach.

Shanghai's industrial concentration areas are on both sides of the Huangpu River and Suzhou Creek. As industrial plants like power plants,

coal transportation, and warehouses were relocated from the city center to the outskirts, the remaining industrial plants along these rivers presented numerous possibilities for transformation. Simultaneously, the emergence of industrial heritage value assessment provides practical guidance for the future conversion of these factories. The most common modes for transformation include preserving factory buildings with strong structural integrity and repurposing them into large-scale spaces like exhibition halls. Industrial parks can be renovated into creative hubs for offices and commercial activities, or transformed into art parks where artist studios and galleries are concentrated. For areas with ample empty space or a large number of factory buildings suitable for demolition, their conversion into open spaces or recreational parks is recommended, offering opportunities for leisure and relaxation.

In the aforementioned modes, the urban regeneration along both sides of the Huangpu River emerged as a prominent large-scale project in Shanghai, achieving the desired

clustering effect. Since the establishment of the Shanghai Pujiang Office in 2001, the transformation of both sides of the Huangpu River from industrial areas to public leisure spaces, green areas, and parks has shaped Shanghai's urban regeneration into a benchmark for other major cities in the country.

Since 2008, Shanghai West Bund, which is located in Xuhui District, has embraced the concept of a "people's city" and adhered to development principles that prioritize leading planning, culture, ecology, and science and technology. Leveraging the opportunities presented by the 2010 World Expo and the connection of the Huangpu River, Shanghai West Bund initiated the regeneration of urban form and public spaces, transforming from an "industrial rust belt" into a vibrant "life show belt" and "tech innovation embroidery belt." In 2012, the Shanghai West Bund Development (Group) Co., Ltd., a state-owned enterprise group, was established and entrusted by the People's Government of Xuhui District to undertake the comprehensive development and construction of the West Bund area.

Over the next decade, West Bund developed the largest art district in Asia and hosted events such as the Shanghai International Artwork Trading Month, the World Artificial Intelligence Conference, and the Shanghai International Financial Center Development Forum. Throughout the process of transforming riverside land into urban development zones, renowned architectural and landscape design firms such as David Chipperfield, SANAA, Atelier FCJZ, Hassell, Sasaki, and others were invited to contribute.

Driven by the renovations of industrial plants along the Huangpu River, Shanghai's urban regeneration has adopted flexible and diverse approaches. Since 2014, Shanghai has issued urban regeneration policies tailored to different types of land use, including industrial land, commercial land, and historical and cultural areas. The city has also explored the mode of independent regeneration by involving the original rights-holders. In terms of planning policies, Shanghai allows the provision of public elements (public space or facilities) in exchange for adjustments in the land use,

height of buildings, and floor areas. In terms of land policies, innovative approaches such as re-distribution of land income, land integration and replacement, land premiums, and registration of real estate have been proposed. In 2021, the release of the Shanghai Urban Regeneration Regulations marked a significant milestone, as it systematizes and legalizes the previously scattered regeneration policies. This move established an integrated urban regeneration system in terms of laws and regulations, and it combined policies with technology that encompasses all the aspects in the entire process of redevelopment.

The Shanghai Urban Space Art Season (SUSAS) held in Xuhui Binjiang in 2015 had "Urban Regeneration" as its theme, and it featured four dedicated sections discussing universal issues, and showcasing acts and cases related to urban renewal. The focus was on urban regeneration centered on industrial heritage on both sides of the Huangpu River, which is now evolving into new art and cultural industries. The art museums in the area were primarily led by state-owned platforms, including PSA,

West Bund Art Museum, Shanghai Modern Art Museum (primarily owned by Shanghai Emerald Art Development Co., Ltd.), and the Museum of Art Pudong. Additionally, there were museums primarily led by private capital, such as Long Museum and Yuz Museum.

Shanghai's urban renewal strategy selected numerous old industrial factories and ruins, some of which have the potential to be promoted as industrial heritage. Unlike the challenges faced in high-density old urban areas, this kind of urban renewal is much less difficult, as a significant number of industrial heritage sites can be transformed into non-residential areas like offices and art parks. For example, Atelier Deshaus' three landmark projects demonstrate the success of this operating model. The Long Museum, the Shanghai Modern Art Museum, and the Riverside Passage, located in three different districts facing the Huang River, are all transformed from industrial structures such as coal bunkers. As art museum operators enter these renovated or newly built art museums, the original industrial factory structures provide

Atelier Deshaus, Shanghai Modern Art Museum
©Tian

long-span spaces with adaptability to meet various curatorial needs. The surrounding areas of the art museums, once factories, have been transformed into open and green spaces, offering citizens places to relax. The integration of art and public spaces marks the most significant change brought by this mode of culture-driven riverside urban regeneration to both sides of the Huangpu River and Suzhou Creek in the past decade, further enhancing conditions for attracting investment.

David Chipperfield Architects, West Bund Museum
©Simon Menges

TM Studio, Urbancross Gallery
©TM Studio

Urban Micro-Regeneration in Shanghai Communities and Neighborhood

We must also acknowledge that the aforementioned urban regeneration projects, which are led by the Shanghai municipal and district-level governments in collaboration with large-scale developers, do not represent the entirety of Shanghai's urban development over the past decade. In the central city, a unique form of urban micro-regeneration has emerged, characterized by Shanghai's distinctive features. We generally define urban micro-regeneration through the lens of urban planning and social public services. Usually, it involves the improvement and enhancement of small-scale public spaces or facilities through renovation, repair, and partial improvements instead of major reconstruction. This approach is undertaken with the objective of serving the needs of the neighborhood and community without increasing construction capacity.

The practice of urban and community small-scale and micro-space regeneration has attracted increasing involvement from designers, and lies at the core of the urban economy, social function, and everyday life of residents. As Michel de Certeau mentions,

everydayness is the witness of the mass culture; urban micro-regeneration captures the moments of citizens' everyday life. Given the historical context filled with contradictions, the adoption of a gradual and gentle update approach is inevitable, considering economic investment and actual operation. The enhancement of the function and quality of these spaces directly influences the overall appearance and value of the city, as well as the well-being that people experience in their everyday life.

Shanghai Clover Nature School, a non-profit organization established in 2014 by Liu Yuelai, a teacher from the Landscape Department of Tongji University, along with architects Fan Haoyang and Wei Min, has been engaged to promote nature conservation and social participation in urban micro-spaces. Putting forward the concept of community gardening, this project focuses on utilizing the inner gardens of old communities and urban residual spaces. Residents come together to create shared community gardens where they grow fruit, vegetables, and flowers. This

participatory approach to micro landscape transformation fosters a sense of collective responsibility toward urban ecology and promotes a sustainable way of life. In this way, a true community culture is formed in this operating mechanism.

In Shanghai's old communities, the addition of sports facilities and service centers for the elderly has become a fundamental livelihood project in recent years. As part of the national initiative to promote fitness for all, the Shanghai Municipal Sports Bureau has installed sports facilities for old communities, but many of these facilities consist of off-the-shelf equipment and lack creativity. In 2021, coinciding with the opening of the Tokyo Olympics, Xiaohongshu (literally meaning "little red book"), a popular fashion app among young people in China, sponsored and successfully completed the reconstruction of sports facilities in two old communities. The renovation adopted bright colors as the theme, using color blocks that appeal to young people on the ground and walls. These two urban micro-regeneration projects have become viral, gaining popularity

Archimixing, Pocket Plaza on Yongjia Road
©Archimixing

Enhanced sports culture in Shanghai neighborhoods
©Jiawei Jiang

as internet celebrity projects. Sports culture in Shanghai neighborhoods gets a boost through these projects.

Through innovative and creative approaches, many of the newly emerging urban micro-regeneration projects have contributed to a vibrant and dynamic urban environment and breathed new life into these communities. Many of the chief designers of such projects may not be widely known, but it is still evident that an increasing number of well-known Shanghai independent architects, who were originally focused on art museums, schools, and industrial parks, are now turning their attention toward urban micro-regeneration. Two firms that stand out in this shift are TM Studio and Archimixing.

TM Studio, led by architect Tong Ming, has undertaken successful projects such as the Urbancross Gallery on Donghu Road and Guizhou Road. After the first round of trial-and-error in regeneration, Urbancross Gallery transferred to the ground floor of the Wukang

Building and established itself as a non-profit organization, exemplifying a collaboration of architect with local neighborhood offices that infuses culture into micro-regeneration initiatives. Similarly, Archimixing has made its mark by designing Pocket Plaza on Yongjia Road, a small square enclosed with open galleries, and attracting café operators to the space. These urban micro-regeneration projects, which have been previously promoted in *Architecture China*, exemplify how cultural enhancement can be incorporated to enliven the community atmosphere. In this issue, it is imperative to revisit these small-scale projects that demonstrate the power of cultural enrichment in fostering a more vibrant and cohesive urban environment.

Through a brief review of two culture-driven urban regeneration models in Shanghai over the past decade, we have observed the transformation of old industrial factories into art galleries, industrial parks, and public spaces for citizens. Simultaneously, the city's old Lilong housings and communities are undergoing

urban micro-regeneration. These projects have been successful and have breathed new life into these areas. As the COVID-19 epidemic gradually recedes from people's daily life in China, we anticipate the emergence of new human-centric regeneration mechanisms in Shanghai's next phase of urban development. With the lessons learned and experiences gained from the past projects, we hope to witness even more innovative and inclusive initiatives that cater to the diverse needs of Shanghai's residents. The continuous pursuit of sustainable and culturally enriched urban development will undoubtedly contribute to a more vibrant and harmonious city.

Xitang Market Gallery

Scenic Architecture Office

Location: 588 Zhenguan Road, Xitang County, Jiashan, Zhejiang Province
Architect: Scenic Architecture Office
Principal architect: Zhu Xiaofeng
Design team: Zhuang Xinjia, Pi Liming, Lin Xiaosheng, Wang Junyuan
Structure consultant: AND Office
Landscape design: TOPO Design Group
Area: 2,500 square meters
Design and construction period: 2018–2021
Photography: Liang Shan

Site plan

The Xitang East Area under construction is the eastward expansion of the old town of Xitang, including nearly 100,000 square meters of tourist retail, hotel, visitor center, and cultural facilities. After completion, it will become a new entrance at the northeast of the old town. Xitang East Area is divided by a river into two phases. As the key point of Phase II, Building One is located at the southwest corner of the northern site, facing the river on the west and south sides to overlook the old town, and adjoining the Phase I retail blocks on the other side of the river.

The old town of Xitang has strict urban planning requirements for the new buildings in the scenic area. In addition to the height limit, sloping roof, small blue-black tile, black and white and gray tone, and wood color are all prerequisites for the design. What kind of program should be planned in the core

area of the East Area riverfront? What kind of form-type should be used to meet the needs of function and establish it as a landmark while complying with the requirements of townscape? It is the answer to these challenges that dominate the entire design process.

The basic urban fabric of the pedestrian streets in East Area is the retail courtyard on the ground and first floors, and gable-roof hotel courtyard on the second floor. On top of this base are the special landmarks scattered in the area, such as the tourist center at the center, the Nijigen Activity Hall at the northeast corner, and the Naera Boutique Hotel at the northwest corner. As one of these landmarks, Building One needs to attract people to stay and participate in proposed activities, thereby forming an agglomeration effect and becoming the highlight of the tourist experience in the entire eastern area. After thorough studies and

discussions, a mixed function of market and art gallery became the consensus of the client and the design team—an open and flowing market space on the first floor to accommodate the organic farmers' market, creative bookstore, coffee shop, restaurant, and hotel reception, with a multifunctional art gallery on the second floor to host exhibitions, forums, and cocktail parties.

Aerial view from the south

Aerial view from the south-west

View from river

View toward the south elevation

Terrace on the first floor

Interior of the first floor

Interior of the first floor

Interior view facing north

Staircase on the first floor

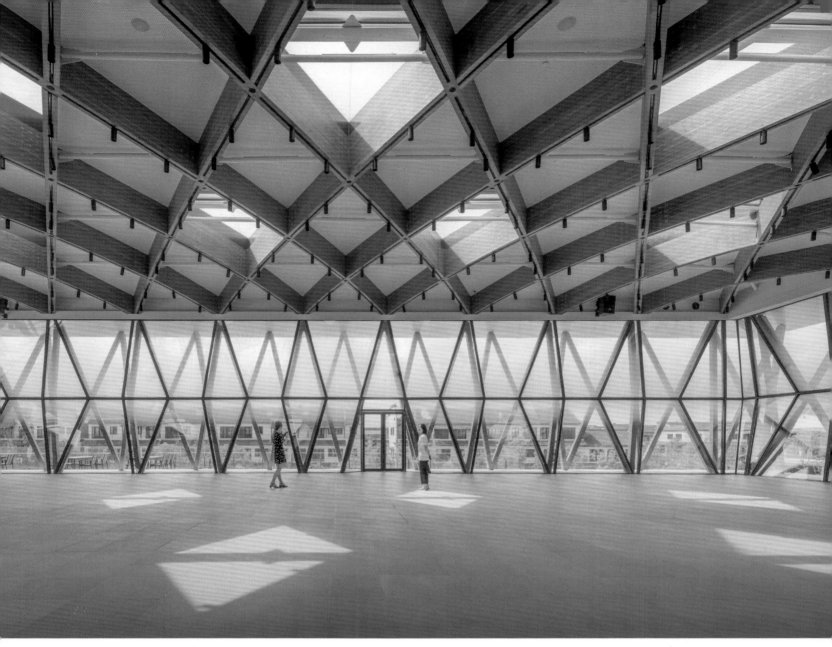

Roof of wooden structure on the upper floor

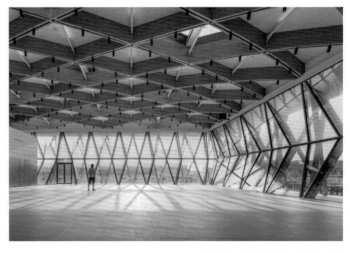

Wooden structure with curtain wall

East elevation

Interior view facing west

Structural details of wooden beams and glazing

We translated the program and style regulations into the design commitment of space and image, which became the basis for the construction. As per the obvious difference between the programs of the upper and lower floors, we continued the stacking pattern of frame and gable roof structure used in the street, but turned it upside-down with the gable roof structure at the bottom in order to display individuality while still coordinating with the whole.

The Chinese overhanging gable roof supported by the white gable wall is a traditional residential form-type in the southern Yangtze River Delta, and a single roof can be replicated continuously to cover a larger area. We extracted the structural form of Y-shaped columns from the geometry of the continuous gable wall to support the upside-down triangular truss roof, forming a linear unit with a width of 6.3 meters and a length of nearly 52 meters. The space in the truss is used to install MEP equipment, and a continuous undulating indoor space is formed under the truss. Six linear units are connected parallel to form the roof covering the ground-floor market, echoing the continuous ancient town settlements. The freely distributed Y-shaped columns ensure open and flowing space for the market, creating a sharable and flexible space for diverse functions. At the east and west ends, some of the Y-shaped columns are replaced by V-shaped gable walls with diagonal braces inside, which solve the seismic force problem and establishe a connection with the traditional gable walls with inverted slopes.

Structural details of wood joints

Roof plan

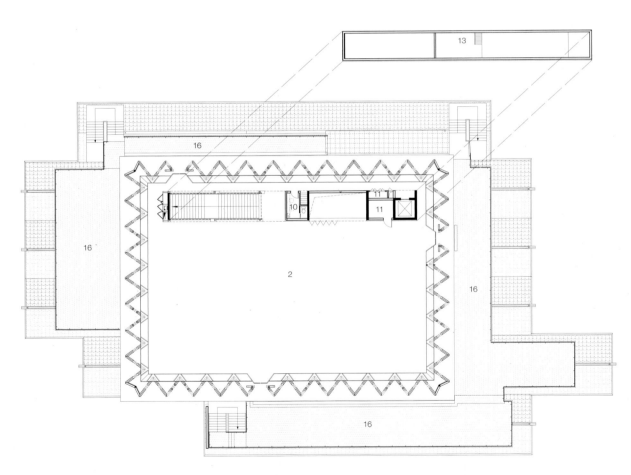

Second-floor plan

First-floor plan

1. Open market space
2. Multi-function space
3. Prep room
4. Restroom
5. Gender-neutral restroom
6. Cleaning room
7. Storage room
8. Pantry
9. Changing room

10. Dressing room
11. Equipment room
12. Lifting platform
13. Equipment platform
14. Porch
15. Verandah
16. Terrace

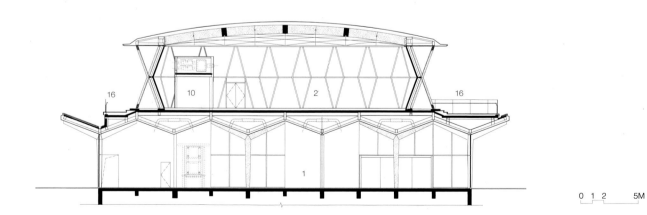

Section A-A

0 1 2   5M

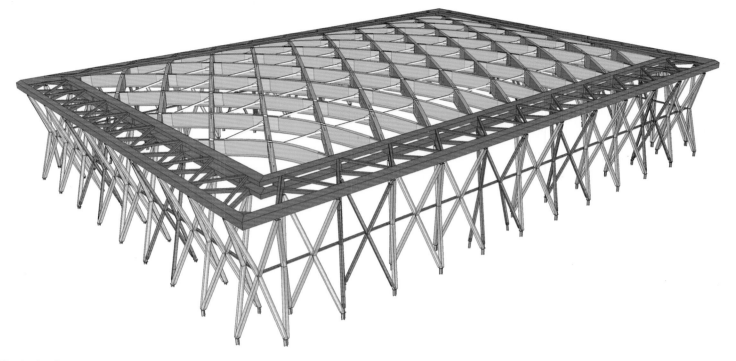

Structural system

Construction of integrated wood and steel structure

Detailed section

1. Aluminum magnesium manganese alloy roofing panel
2. Dark gray aluminum plate
3. White aluminum plate
4. Glulam column (160 by 160 mm)
5. Dark gray T-shaped steel stud curtain wall system
6. Atomized gradient glazed glass
7. Steel rod
8. Bamboo flooring
9. Low-iron laminated tempered glass
10. Blast stainless steel railings
11. Blue-black Chinese-style tile
12. Stainless steel gutter
13. White aluminum plate
14. 20 mm white aluminum honeycomb plate
15. Steel beam
16. Low-iron insulating glass
17. Dark gray T-shaped curtain wall locked cover
18. Fine aggregate concrete solidified floor

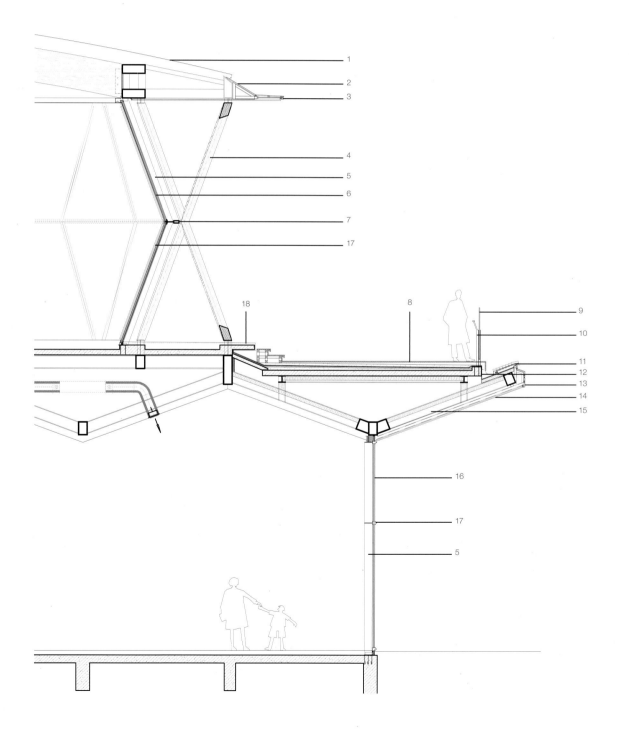

Tag Art Museum

Ateliers Jean Nouvel

Location: 1111 Yinshatan Road, West Coast New Area, Qindao, Shandong Province
Architect: Ateliers Jean Nouvel
Principal architect: Jean Nouvel
Area: 17,000 square meters
Design and construction period: 2012–2021
Photography: Huang Shaoli, Chao Qixuan

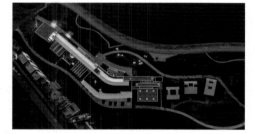

Satellite view

On the bank of Tangdao Bay in Qingdao West Coast New Area, TAG Art Museum extends along the coastline embraced by the Phoenix Island Tourism Resort, which is praised as "a coastal tourism resort with the most superior resources along the whole coastline of China" by the World Tourism Organization.

TAG Art Museum is a non-profit art institution located in The Artists' Garden, an international comprehensive art community. The museum, based on the concept of echoing community art ecology with architecture and garden, was designed by Jean Nouvel, a famous French architect, and jointly built with Gilles Clément, a French landscape designer, aiming at helping urban development with contemporary art.

TAG Art Museum, covering a land area of 5,837.5 square meters, and with a building area of 17,000 square meters, is composed of twelve professional exhibition halls built by the sea; exclusive art spaces such as a music auditorium, a viewing hall, and art workshops; leisure consumption spaces such as TAG·Cafe, TAG·Bar, TAG·Store, TAG·Garden, and TAG·Port; as well as member-exclusive spaces for social activities.

Fusion with the City

Considering the style and characteristics of the urban buildings of Qingdao, European architects are entrusted to continue the urban architectural context at the TAG Art Museum, and express and strengthen the artistic attributes of the art museum with originality, uniqueness, and artistry of architecture.

Jean Nouvel proposes that "every building is alive, unique and special, and should be in harmony with its surroundings and the spirit of the place." TAG Art Museum, based on the locality, emphasizes the connection and full respect for the spirit of the place, in a bid to fully integrate the architecture with the cultural and natural environment.

Its twelve exhibition halls are connected yet relatively independent, showing different forms and inclusiveness. With a variety of architectural structures and volumes, exquisite light application, and unique exhibition conditions, they can satisfy the exhibition of both classical and contemporary art works, enable curators to release their wisdom to the maximum extent, and fully stimulate the creative inspiration of the artists, thus providing the public with fresh artistic experience and spatial feeling. The exhibition halls in various forms are not simply spliced by objects, and Nouvel roots his understanding of art in continuity and constructs it in space.

Overall aerial view

Landscape designed by Gilles Clément

Curtain wall

Anodized aluminum sheets reflect the natural environment

Architecture Shuttling Between Light and Shadow

To present every detail perfectly, TAG Art Museum has done many R&D experiments with relevant institutions, and more than twenty systems have been developed independently, such as the lifting ceiling and exterior shading system of No. 5 Exhibition Hall, and the mobile acoustic reflector system of the music auditorium. Moreover, Nouvel applies a large number of new materials in architecture, to form a unique architectural concept by fully integrating the elements of nature, tradition, modernity, and technology.

Large anodized aluminum sheets are used for the curtain wall of the museum, which not only boast improved hardness and wear resistance, but also good heat resistance and excellent insulation. The oxide film formed on the sheet surface is protective and decorative, without any paint coating, so as to better adapt to the climate environment of the seaside while highlighting the modern sense of metal color. In order to avoid color difference and improve corrosion resistance, all anodized aluminum products used for the curtain wall are custom-made and imported from Austria.

Main entrance

Electric sunshade louvers enclosing No. 5 Exhibition Hall

Interior of No. 5 Exhibition Hall

Art installation

Interior of exhibition hall

The atrium of No. 3 Exhibition Hall enclosed by glass

The light and shadow in building materials are applied to the extreme. The curtain walls of various materials construct spatial images mixed with reality and virtuality, and the building surfaces blend with the blue sky, sea, and plants in between the back-turning light. Seen from the outside of the building, the flowing clouds, sunset, and sky are reproduced from a new angle. The objects and images between light and shadow are overlapped into a flowing picture, and the spatial relationship of the plane is reconstructed to form the scenery image of "picture in picture," which expands the perception of art to another dimension.

Landscape of Internal and External Interaction

Four windows of No. 7 and No. 8 Halls are opened to the sea side. The aspect ratio and elevational position of the rectangles are different, of which the former is determined based on the scale ratio of traditional Chinese landscape paintings, allowing unreserved unfolding of the views of the mountain and sea of Tangdao Bay. Through the exquisite design of window angle, the distant scene is inverted in front of the eyes, creating a kaleidoscope visual experience. Curtains waken the light and create a hazy mood of painting.

As light pours into the interior from the roof of No. 3 Hall, the vitality in the morning, the brightness in the noon, and the warmth in the evening all fall into this circular space. The central atrium is enclosed by glass, which is not connected with the interior of the exhibition hall. The view of visitors can pass through the plant landscape to the sky, allowing the consciousness to flow freely between the artistic works and the natural background.

The corridors between the exhibition halls are mostly enclosed by glass. Walking among the twelve rich and orderly exhibition halls, visitors find mountains, sea, gardens, and the city introduced into the art museum through a new space combination. The interaction between exhibits, buildings, nature, and city continues during the viewing, providing the audience with a space for precipitation of the mind during viewing intervals. People move in space, and light changes with time. Space and time thus overlap, casting shadows of varying depths, becoming an experimental art of interaction between nature and viewers.

Interior of exhibition hall

Interior of exhibition hall

Interior of No. 6 Exhibition Hall

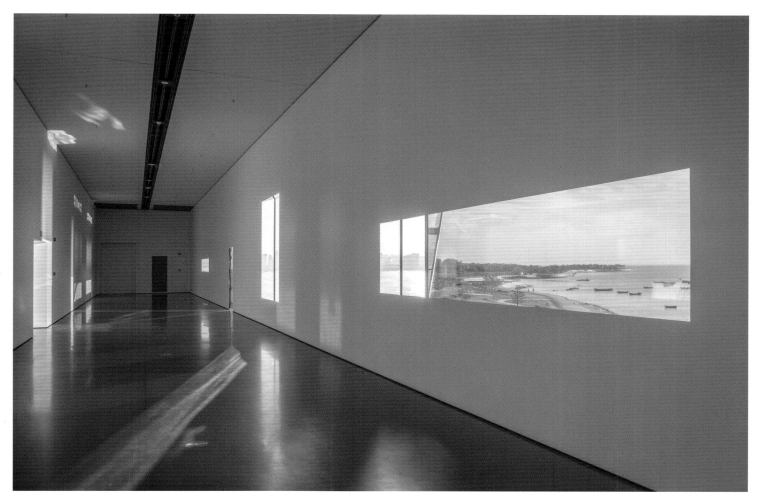

View from No. 7 Exhibition Hall

View from the corridors

Interior of No. 9 Exhibition Hall

Anodized aluminum sunshade panels hung outside the "100m gallery"

Details of aluminum panels

First-floor plan

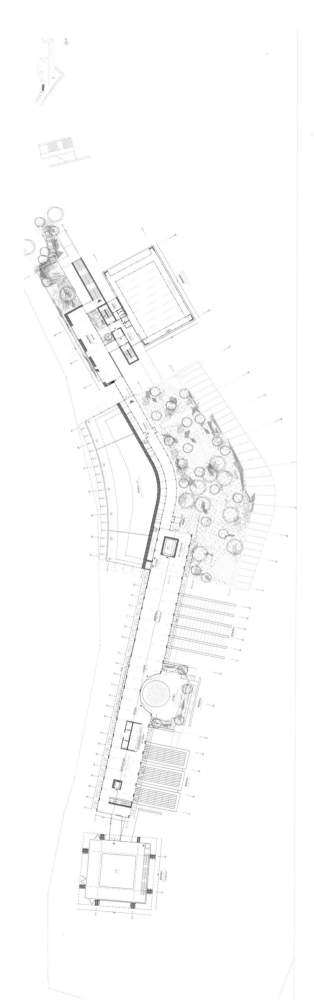

Second-floor plan

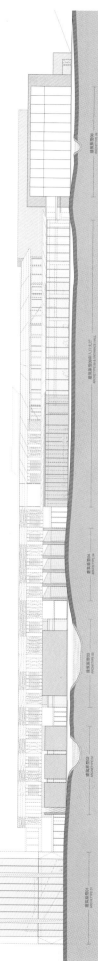

East elevation

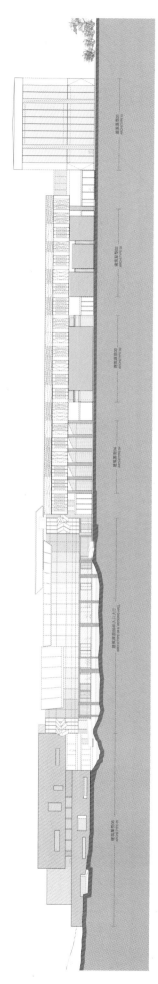

West elevation

Jingdezhen Imperial Kiln Museum

Studio Zhu Pei

Location: East gate of Royal Kiln Factory, Shengli Road and Zhonghua North Road, Jingdezhen, Jiangxi Province
Architect: Zhu Pei
Design team: Shuhei Nakamura, He Fan, Han Mo, You Changchen, Zhang Shun, Liu Yian, Liu Ling, Wu Zhigang, Du Yang, Yang Shengchen, Chen Yida, He Chenglong, Ding Xinyue, Nie Wenhao
Structural consultant: Architectural Design & Research Institute of Tsinghua University
Critic: Zhou Rong
Art consultant: Wang Mingxian, Li Xiangning
Area: 10,370 square meters
Design period: 2015–2016
Construction period: 2017–2020
Photography: Schranimage, Tian Fangfang, Studio Zhu Pei

Site plan

Context

The porcelain museum focusing on imperial kiln artifacts is located in the center of the historical area in Jingdezhen, adjacent to the Imperial Kiln Ruins of the Ming Dynasty. It is surrounded by various historical buildings, including old houses, traditional kilns, factories, and residential buildings of the late 1990s. Those buildings have shaped a rich and diverse urban fabric and formed a unique site with enriching historical contexts.

Site model

Aerial view

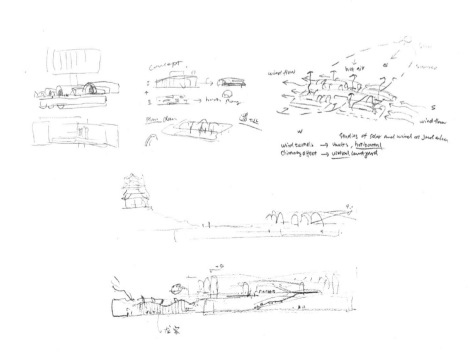

Sketch

View to auditorium and sunken courtyard

The main entrance

Concept

The concept of the Imperial Kiln Museum focuses on rediscovering the roots of Jingdezhen and the innovation ideas that define the revolutionary thinking of the museum experience.

Prototype

As an essential structure for the city's industrial production and as a central place for both public life and cultural memory, the brick kiln has entered the city's history as an architectural form. The prototype of the museum is translated from traditional brick kiln; it comprises more than half a dozen brick vaults based on the traditional form of the kilns. Each of the brick vaults is a different size, length, and curvature, calling to mind the special and material quality of the kilns. The ground level and lower level connect all vaults and courtyards with a strong local cultural grounding.

A porous installation of wind

Jingdezhen is hot in summer, people have to survive under shade with ventilation, and this is the reason why a narrow alley with a roof overhang and small vertical courtyard house create shade and wind tunnels to help people feel comfortable.

The long axis of eight brick vaults is arranged along the north–south axis with the ends open. The arrangement of the open vault and enclosed ones, can not only block the sunlight on the west side, but also transform each vault into a wind tunnel, allowing the cool breeze to flow in and to capture the north–south wind in summer. The five sunken courtyards of different scales create the chimney effect as in the local vertical courtyards. A 3D wind installation is thus created by both the tunnels where wind blows horizontally, and the chimney effect that functions vertically.

An installation of natural light

Constructing an interior space that is full of natural light is the primary consideration. First of all, the alternative arrangement of open vaults and enclosed vaults creates a rhythmic sensation of light and shade while walking through the museum. Secondly, the five sunken courtyards channel light down to the floor, completely subverting people's feelings of the underground space. Moreover, the interior natural light is achieved through the opening of both the end of the vaults, the horizontal slits alongside the floor, the slits between adjacent two vaults, and the cylindrical skylights. With all these special "windows" and the porosity of the building, light diffuses into the interior space of the museum through different dimensions and ways. Natural light is a medium that weaves people, exhibits, and architecture together.

Foyer

Foyer with porcelain installations

Foyer with porcelain installations

View from the amphitheater to Ming porcelain ruins

Sunken courtyards bring natural light to the exhibition hall

Permanent exhibition on the underground level

View to the foyer of the auditorium

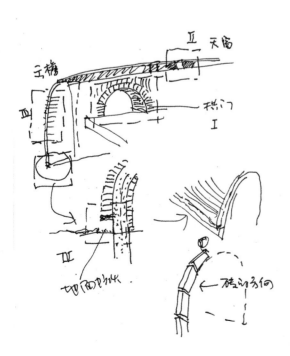

1. this museum is inspired by local historical kiln.

Sketch

Atrium

View to the foyer of the auditorium

Vault, brick, and light

View from the exhibition hall to the amphitheater

Structure and Materials

The basic structure of the museum is an arched structure system; it is made up of concrete poured in between two layers of masonry brick walls.

Using recycled kiln bricks to build a house is a significant character in Jingdezhen because kilns have to be demolished every two or three years in order to keep a certain thermal performance. The recycled old kiln bricks are mixed with new bricks together to reflect the local culture of construction.

This interweaving of nature, ruins, wind, light, sound, and new and old materials must arouse interest and curiosity, create new questions, and give new answers by interacting with the minds of people who inevitably evoke memories and enjoy a unique experience. The past cannot be erased, but can be rewritten by recounting, with a new awareness and maturity, a sort of contemporary archeology.

Sunken courtyard

Clockwise from top left:
Old kiln bricks with glaze;
View to tearoom;
Sunken courtyard;
Brick details

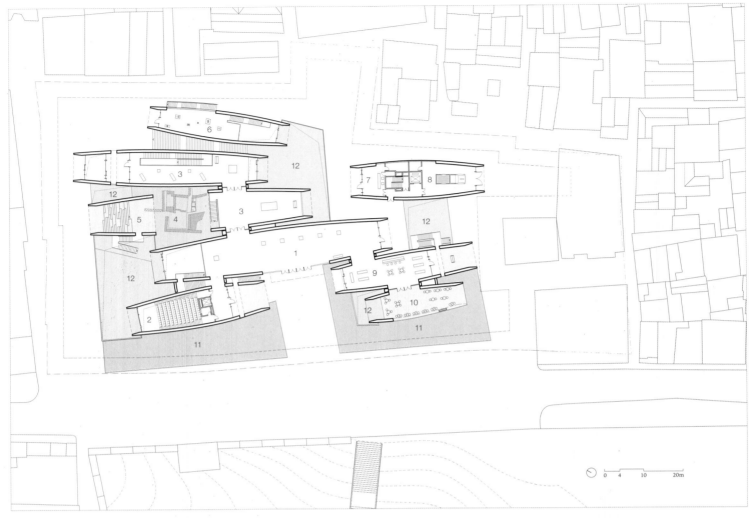

Ground-floor plan

1. Foyer
2. Auditorium
3. Permanent exhibition
4. Ruins
5. Amphitheater
6. Temporary exhibition
7. Office lobby
8. Loading dock
9. Bookstore and café
10. Tearoom
11. Pool
12. Sunken courtyard

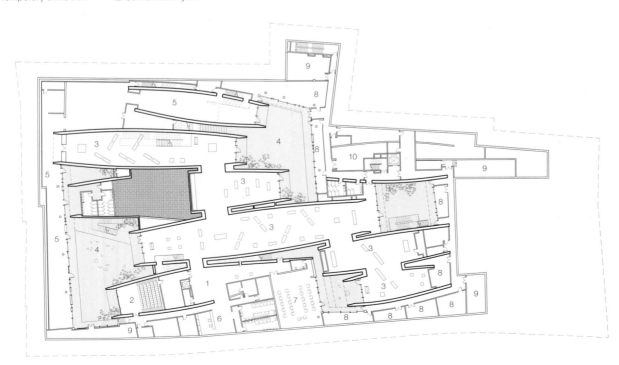

Underground floor plan

1. Foyer
2. Auditorium
3. Permanent exhibition
4. Sunken courtyard
5. Temporary exhibition
6. Coat check
7. Multifunction hall
8. Restoration room
9. Mechanical room
10. Storage

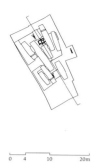

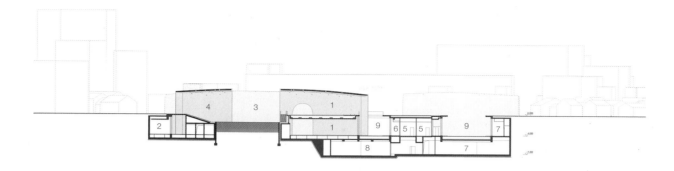

Section A-A

1. Permanent exhibition
2. Temporary exhibition
3. Ruins
4. Amphitheater
5. Restroom

6. Restoration room
7. Storage
8. AC room
9. Sunken courtyard

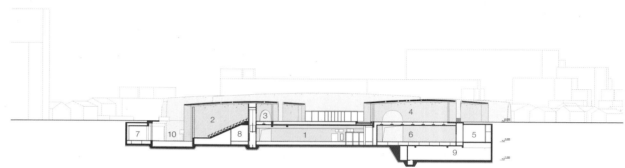

Section B-B

1. Foyer
2. Auditorium
3. Lobby of auditorium
4. Bookstore and café
5. Mechanical room

6. Permanent exhibition
7. Temporary exhibition
8. AC room
9. Storage
10. Sunken courtyard

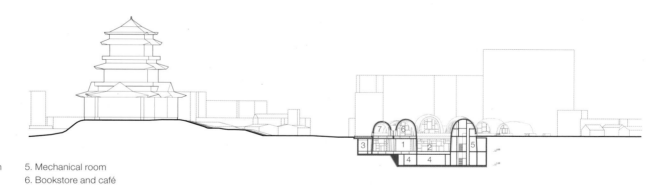

Section C-C

1. Permanent exhibition
2. Sunken courtyard
3. Restoration room
4. Storage

5. Mechanical room
6. Bookstore and café
7. Tearoom

West elevation

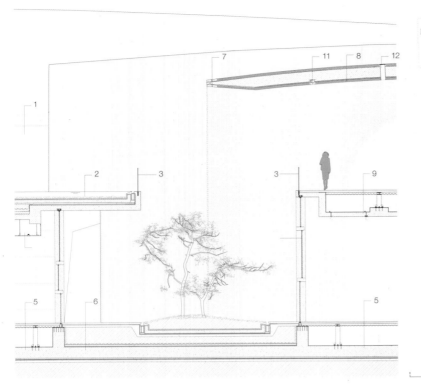

Detail A: Construction system vertical section

1. Faced concrete lintel of 300-mm-height,
   400-mm-wide brushed stainless steel door frame,
   8+1.52PVB+8 ultra white tempered laminated glass
2. Water
   50-mm black pebble with grain size of 50-70 mm,
   600-by-600-by-30-mm gray granite,
   20-mm 1:3 cement mortar binding layer,
   150-mm reinforced concrete pool
3. Tempered laminated glass fence 6+1.52PVB+6
4. 90-by-40-mm Aluminum C-profile framing suspended
   by tie rods,
   12-mm flame-retardant panel,

12-mm moisture-resistant gypsum board,
white oak veneer
5. 40-mm granite floor,
   60-mm 1:3 dry hard cement mortar bonding layer,
   steel corrugated plate and 100-mm concrete pouring,
   equipment interlayer,
   10-mm 1:2 cement mortar protective layer,
   one 1.5-mm waterproof mortar, Cement-based
   penetrating crystalline,
   P6 impermeable reinforced concrete floor
6. 80-mm granite floor,
   30-mm 1:3 dry hard cement mortar bonding layer,
   100-mm C15 plain concrete cushion,
   pain soil compaction,

200 g/m³ non woven filter layer, concave-convex
drainage board,
70-mm C20 fine stone concrete protective layer,
0.4-mm polyethylene plastic film insulation,
waterproof layer: 4+3 thick poly cool tire SBS
modified bitumen waterproof membrane,
20-mm cement mortar leveling layer.
The thinnest part is 40-mm-thick aerated fragmented
concrete 1% slope finding layer,
P6 impermeable reinforced concrete floor
7. Kiln brick 230-by-30-by-60-mm masonry, 30-mm 1:2
   cement mortar,
   one 1.5-mm waterproof mortar,
   cement-based penetrating crystalline,
   P6 impermeable reinforced concrete structure ends
   thinning,
   30-mm 1:2 cement mortar,
   kiln brick 230-by-30-by-60-mm masonry
8. New and old kiln brick 230-by-30-by-60-mm masonry,
   30-mm 1:2 cement mortar,
   one 1.5mm waterproof mortar,
   cement-based penetrating crystalline,
   P6 impermeable reinforced concrete structure ,
   60-mm dry hard insulation rock wool board,
   30-mm 1:2 cement mortar,
   kiln brick 230-by-30-by-60-mm masonry
9. 40-mm granite floor,
   60-mm 1:3 dry hard cement mortar bonding layer,
   Steel corrugated plate and 100-mm concrete pouring,
   equipment interlayer,
   10-mm 1:2 cement mortar protective layer,
   one 1.5-mm waterproof mortar,
   cement-based penetrating crystalline,
   reinforced concrete floor with fair-faced concrete
   bottom
10. Solid wood keel,
    6+1.14PVB+6+12A+8-mm laminated hollow tempered
    glass
11. Lighting lamps
12. 200-mm-diameter, stainless-steel skylight tube

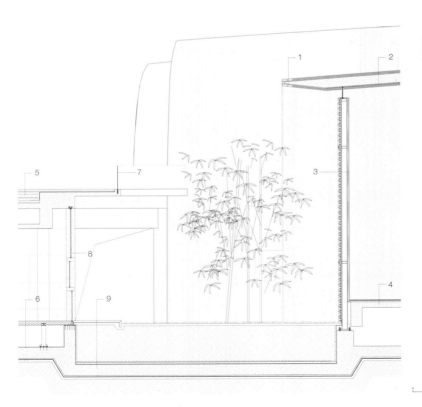

Detail B: Construction system vertical section

1. Kiln brick 230-by-30-by-60-mm masonry,
   30-mm 1:2 cement mortar,
   one 1.5-mm waterproof mortar,
   cement-based penetrating crystalline,
   P6 impermeable reinforced concrete structure ends
   thinning,
   30-mm 1:2 cement mortar,
   kiln brick 230-by-30-by-60-mm masonry
2. New and old kiln brick
   230-by-30-by-60-mm masonry,
   30-mm 1:2 cement mortar,
   one 1.5-mm waterproof mortar,
   cement-based penetrating crystalline,
   P6 impermeable reinforced concrete structure,
   60-mm dry hard insulation rock wool board,
   30-mm 1:2 cement mortar,
   kiln brick 230-by-30-by-60-mm masonry
3. Dry hanging kiln bricks,
   size 230-by-30-by-60-mm,
   aluminum alloy hanging code profile,
   30-by-30-by-4-mm aluminum-alloy square tube,
   vertical steel keel,
   metal waterproof board,
   indoor sound-absorbing panel

4. 8-mm tongue-and-groove laminate flooring,
   5-mm foam padding,
   15-mm pine wool bottom plate 45° diagonal laying,
   20-mm I: 2.5 cement mortar leveling,
   50-mm LC7.5 lightweight aggregate concrete,
   reinforced concrete floor
5. 80-mm granite floor,
   30-mm 1:3 dry hard cement mortar bonding layer,
   100-mm Cl5 plain concrete cushion,
   plain soil compaction
6. 40-mm granite floor,
   60-mm 1:3 dry hard cement mortar bonding layer,

corrugated-steel plate and 100mm concrete pouring,
   equipment interlayer,
   10-mm 1:2 cement mortar protective layer,
   one 1.5-mm waterproof mortar,
   cement-based penetrating crystalline,
   P6 impermeable reinforced concrete floor
7. Tempered laminated glass fence 6 + 1.5PVB + 6
8. Solid wood keel,
   6+1.14PVB+6+12A+8-mm laminated hollow tempered glass
9. 80-mm granite floor,
   30-mm 1:3 dry hard cement mortar bonding layer,

100-mm Cl5 plain concrete cushion,
   plain soil compaction,
   200 g/m³ non woven filter layer,
   concave-convex drainage board,
   70-mm C20 fine stone concrete protective layer,
   0.4-mm polyethylene plastic film isolation layer,
   waterproof layer: 4+3 thick poly cool tire SBS modified bitumen waterproof membrane,
   20-mm cement mortar leveling layer.
   The thinnest part is 40-mm-thick aerated fragmented concrete 1% slope finding layer,
   P6 impermeable concrete roof

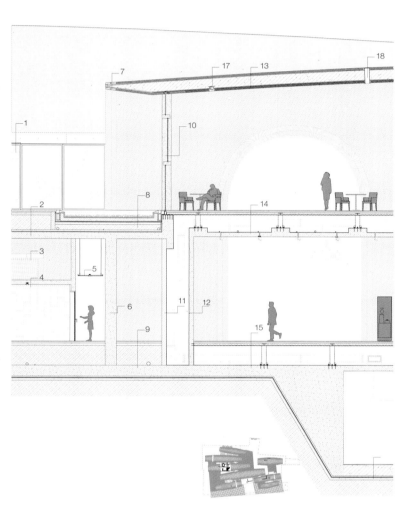

Detail C: Construction system vertical section

1. 300-mm fair-faced concrete beam,
   40-mm brushed stainless-steel canopy,
   40-mm brushed stainless-steel door frame,
   8+1.52PVB+8 laminated ultra white tempered glass
2. 8-mm granite floor,
   30-mm 1:3 dry hard cement mortar bonding layer,
   100-mm screed,
   compaction soil,
   50-mm fine aggregate concrete,
   polyethylene film,
   4+3 double waterproof membrane,
   20-mm 1:2.5 mortar layer,
   P6 impermeable reinforced concrete floor slab,
   with is fair-faced concrete base
3. 200-mm high fair-faced concrete beam,
   solid wood ventilation shutters
4. White waterproof latex paint sprayed on the top,
   aluminum alloy tuyere,

600-by-300-mm white tiles
5. 90-by-40-mm aluminum C-profile framing suspended by tie rods,
   12-mm flame-retardant panel,
   12-mm moisture-resistant,
   white oak
6. Fair-faced concrete wall
7. Kiln brick 230-by-30-by-60-mm masonry,
   30-mm 1:2 mortar layer,
   1.5-mm cement-based infiltration crystallization,
   P6 impervious reinforced concrete structure,
   30-mm 1:2 mortar layer,
   kiln brick 230-by-30-by-60-mm masonry
8. Water
   50-mm thick, 50-70-mm-diameter gray gravel,
   600-by-600-by-30-mm gray granite,
   20-mm 1:3 mortar layer,
   150-mm reinforced concrete pool,
   20-mm 1:3 mortar protective layer,
   2-mm PVC waterproof membrane,

20-mm 1:3 mortar layer,
   100-mm screed,
   rammed earth
9. 40-mm granite floor,
   60-mm 1:3 dry hard cement mortar bonding layer,
   100-mm screed,
   rammed earth,
   P6 impermeable reinforced concrete floor slab
10. Solid wood keel,
    6+1.14PVB+6+12A+8-mm tempered glass
11. Equipment pipeline well,
    5-mm 1:2 mortar protective layer,
    1.5-mm cement-based infiltration crystallization,
    10-mm 1:2 mortar layer,
    240-mm-thick kiln brick wall
12. Reinforced concrete wall with fair-faced concrete inner surface,
    1.5-mm cement-based infiltration crystallization,
    10-mm 1:2 mortar protective layer
13. New and recycled historical kiln brick 230-by-30-by-60-mm masonry,
    30-mm 1:2 mortar layer,
    1.5-mm cement-based infiltration crystallization,
    P6 impervious reinforced concrete structure,
    60-mm dry hard insulation rock wool board,
    30-mm1:2 mortar layer,
    kiln brick 230-by-30-by-60-mm masonry
14. 40-mm granite floor,
    60-mm 1:3 dry hard cement mortar bonding layer,
    40-mm corrugated-steel sheet with 100-mm concrete pouring,
    equipment interlayer,
    10-mm 1:2 mortar protective layer,
    1.5-mm cement-based infiltration crystallization,
    reinforced concrete slab,with fair-faced concrete
15. 40-mm granite floor,
    60-mm 1:3 dry hard cement mortar bonding layer,
    40-mm steel corrugated sheet with 100mm concrete base
    pouring,
    equipment interlayer,
    10-mm 1:2 mortar protective layer,
    1.5-mm cement-based infiltration crystallization,
    P6 impermeable reinforced concrete floor slab
16. 20-mm 1:2 cement mortar surface layer,
    P10 impermeable reinforced concrete floor slab,
    50-mm C20 fine-stone concrete,
    polyethylene film,
    4+3 double waterproof membrane,
    20-mm 1:2.5 mortar layer,
    100-mm screed,
    rammed earth
17. Lighting
18. Brushed stainless-steel skylight tube 200-mm diameter

Qintai Art Museum

Atelier Deshaus

Location: Zhiyin Avenue, Hanyang District, Wuhan, Hubei Province
Architect: Atelier Deshaus
Principal architect: Liu Yichun
Design team: Chen Yu, Wang Longhai, Hu Chenchen, Chen Hao, Shen Wen, Chen Chihhan, Tang Yun, Zhang Xiaoqi, Wu Wenchao, Deng Rui, Liu Xin, Pang Zirui, Wang Jiawen, Cao Ye
Collaboration: Wuhan Architectural Design Institute
Client: Wuhan Urban Construction Group Co.,Ltd.
Floor area: 43,000 square meters
Design and construction period: 2016–2021
Photography: Fangfang Tian, Shengliang Su

Site plan

Qintai Art Museum is located on the lakeside of the Moon Lake in Wuhan's Hanyang district, facing the Meizi Hill across the lake to the south. In order to reduce the weight of the architectural mass on the natural surface of the lake, the form of an undulating natural terrain is used in the direction of the lake, while sinking part of the exhibition spaces underground. This uses the underground space, and also minimizes the mass on the ground. On the side facing the city road, on the other hand, a vertical facade continues to uphold architecture's urbanity.

The undulating roof is formed by an abstract stepped terrace following topographic contours. The risers of the steps are lined with a silver metallic surface, while the treads are covered with white stones and low vegetation, traversed by winding, planked walking paths. These rooftop paths are entirely open to the public, connecting to the Moon Lake, as well as to the exits of the museum exhibition spaces, the space for public education, the art shop, the café, and the other public spaces. Thus, they form a public space framework independent from the exhibition spaces of the museum. The activities of the public are part of the architectural surface.

Closer view to the roof paved by white gravel

Aerial view

Undulating shape facing the lake

View toward the lake

Aerial view of the undulating roof

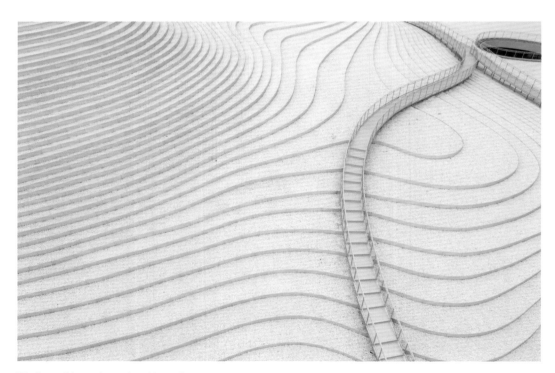

Winding walking paths on the white roof

Details of winding walking paths

Details of staircase

Closer view to the roof paved by white gravel

North facade, reserving space for an urban plaza on the west

View on the walking paths

The art museum architecture as intervention has redefined the urban space on the south bank of Moon Lake. The space to the west of the museum is reserved for an urban plaza, where the planned Wuhan Library and Drama Centre will be. The main entrance to the museum, as well as the programs with strong public tenets including the Creative Cultural Spaces, are all placed on this side, where a subtly inwardly curved facade creates a sense of enclosure. From the plaza, there are ramped paths linking to the second-floor café and rooftop terrace, establishing a public circulation that could still operate after the museum closes. Operationally, this strengthens the openness of the museum and the urbanity of the architecture.

Walking path and the building

Lobby

Unique space under the undulating roof

The undulating roof seen from the interior

Light diffused into the space

The main hall, together with the undulating roofscape, creates a unique space for exhibition. The exhibition space uses floating exhibition walls, and there is no longer a set pathway for visiting the exhibition. The walls are surfaces for exhibiting, as well as providing the structure for the undulating roof. The exhibition spaces for contemporary art, modern art, classical art, as well as for special exhibitions, can be independently accessed, or sequentially linked, providing great functional flexibility.

Details of the roof

Paths toward lobby

Unique space under the undulating roof

Exhibition space under construction

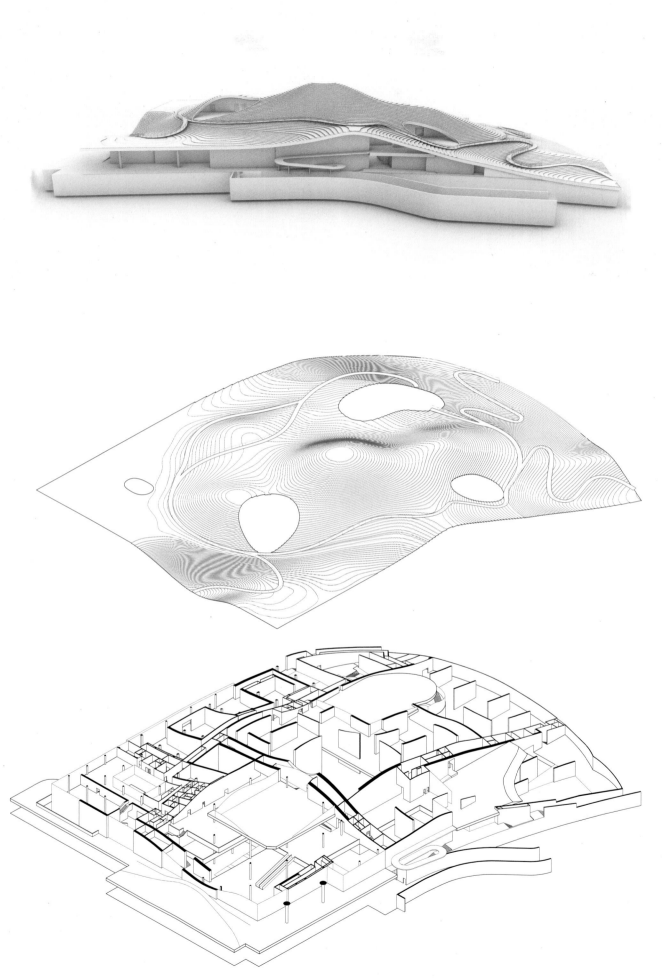

Exploded axonometric view

0 5   25m

First-floor plan

1. Cultural and creative
2. Office
3. Service
4. Equipment
5. Restaurant
6. Kitchen
7. Entrance hall
8. Auditorium
9. Lobby (Contemporary art)
10. Temporary exhibition hall (Contemporary art)

11. Lobby (Modern art)
12. Temporary Exhibition Hall (Modern art)
13. Exhibition Hall (Ancient art)
14. Lobby (Ancient art)
15. Temporary exhibition hall
16. Multifunctional hall
17. VIP room
18. Reading room
19. Café
20. Family activity zone

21. Cultural and creative terrace
22. Exit passageway
23. Underground warehouse
24. Underground parking
25. Terrace
26. East foyer
27. West foyer
28. Underground exhibition hall
29. VIP Exhibition hall
30. Outdoor bicycle parking

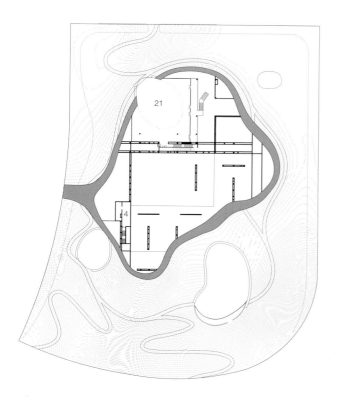

Roof plan

Second-floor plan

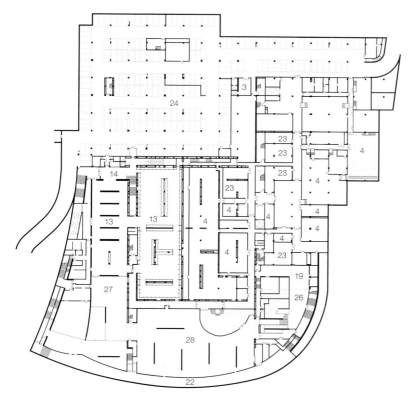

Underground floor plan

Plan of mezzanine

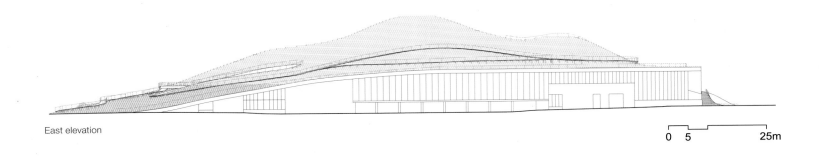

East elevation

0 5   25m

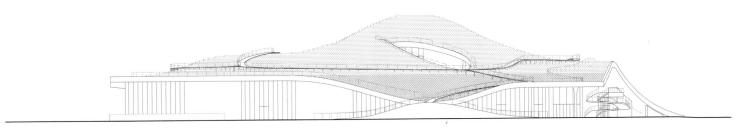

North elevation

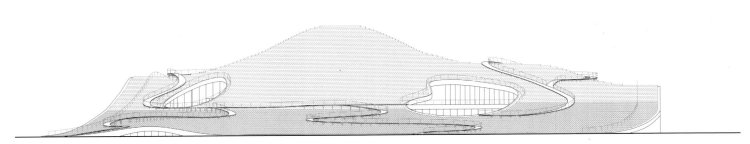

South elevation

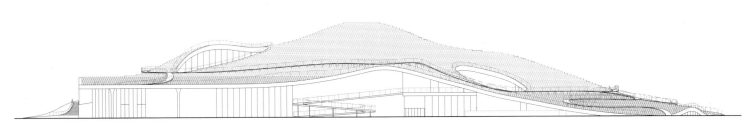

West elevation

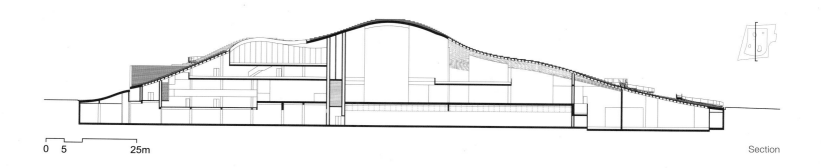

0 5   25m

Section

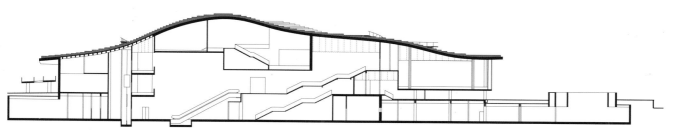

Section

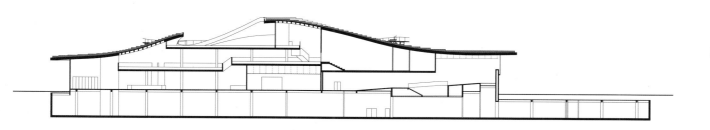

Section

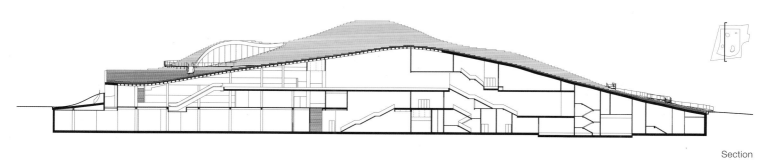

Section

The Cloudscape of Haikou

MAD Architects

Location: Haikou, Hainan Province
Architect: MAD Architects
Principal architects: Ma Yansong, Dang Qun, Yosuke Hayano
Associate in charge: Fu Changrui
Design team: Qiang Siyang, Shang Li, Sun Feifei, Dayie Wu, Alan Rodríguez Carrillo, Xie Qilin, Beatrice Bavuso
Site area: 4,397 square meters
Floor area: 1,380 square meters
Client: Haikou Tourism & Culture Investment Holding Group
Executive architect: East China Architectural Design and Research Institute
Facade consultant: RFR Shanghai
Lighting consultant: Beijing Ning Field Lighting Design Corp., Ltd.
Interior design: Beijing Ling & BuYao Interior design
Construction contractor: Yihuida Shimizu Concrete
Design and construction period: 2019–2021
Photography: Arch-Exist, CreatAR Images, Aogvision

MAD joins this collection of pavilions with a building containing a bookstore and amenities. Situated in Century Park on the shore of Haikou Bay, the project covers an area of 4,397 square meters, with a construction area of 1,380 square meters. To the south side of the pavilion are a library and reading space capable of holding 10,000 books, as well as a multifunctional audio-visual area, which is free and open for public use. Meanwhile, the building's northern area features a café, public restrooms, barrier-free restrooms, showers, a nursery room, a public rest area, and a roof garden.

Beginning a new book is often a moment that readers cherish: a venture into the surreal or unknown and gentle removal from everyday reality. The visiting experience of the Cloudscape is similar. The architecture enables people to approach the building removed from our familiar urban reality, and begin a new journey transcending time and space. The complexity of the cave-shaped form deconstructs the space layer by layer, offering readers a weightless field to be inhabited by their imagination.

Aerial view

View from the sea

The building, quietly located between land and sea, is highly sculptural. The pavilion's free and organic forms also allow for the creation of unique interior spaces, where walls, floors, and ceilings merge in unpredictable ways, and the boundaries between the indoors and outdoors are blurred.

The circular openings of the building are reminiscent of holes forged by wildlife or seas, blurring the boundary between architecture and nature. The varying sizes of the openings allow natural light into the interior and create a natural ventilation effect to cool the building in Haikou's year-round warm climate. Through the holes, people observe the sky and sea, as if looking at a familiar world through the passage of time and space. This layering of atmospheres, and collision between people and space, creates a sense of living ritual.

The cascading reading area facing the sea, which connects the first and second floors, is not exclusively for reading, but also a venue for cultural exchange activities. The children's reading area is isolated from the main reading space, where skylights, holes, and niches stimulate the children's desire to explore.

The structural form creates several semi-outdoor spaces and platforms, which also serve as excellent spaces for people to read and gaze at the sea. In response to the local hot climate, the gray space of the building's outer corridor is cantilevered to achieve comfortable temperatures, culminating in a sustainable, energy-saving structure.

Closer view of the curved shape

View from the reflection pool

Details of fair-faced concrete and glass

Skylights

Openings toward the sea

Skylights viewed from the interior

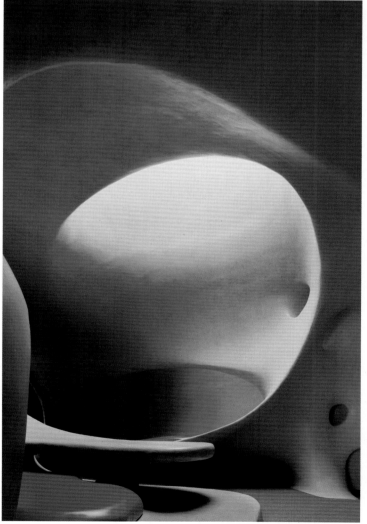

Interior with curved shapes made with fair-faced concrete

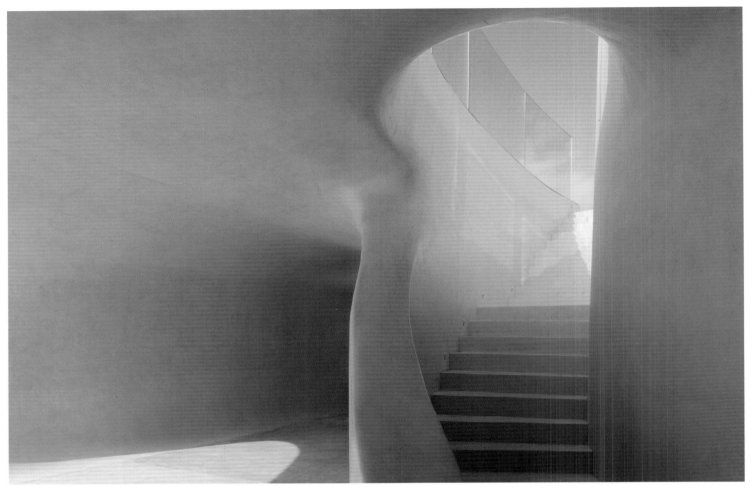

Staircase toward the terrace

Through their pavilion, MAD champions an "anti-material" approach, avoiding the intentional expression of structure and construction, thus dissolving the inherent everyday perception of the material and allowing the spatial feeling itself to become the main subject. Here, concrete is a liquid material, characterized by its flowing, soft, and variable structural form.

The interior and exterior of the building are cast in fair-faced concrete to create a single cohesive, flowing form. The roof and floor feature double-layered waffle slabs that support the building's scale and large cantilever. The design development was conducted and tested using digital models. It was possible to hide all mechanical, electrical, and plumbing elements within the concrete cavity to minimize their appearance and create visual consistency. The smooth, organic aura of the pavilion is only made possible by this key integration of architecture, structure, and mechanical and electrical design. Ma Yansong said:

Spirituality is the core value of architecture. It contributes to the humanistic atmosphere of a city. We want this building to be an urban space that people would like to make part of their daily lives. Architecture, art, humanity, and nature meet here, opening up a journey of visitors' imaginations to explore and appreciate the meaning that different beauties bring to their lives.

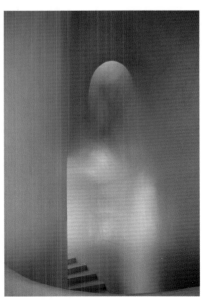

Fair-faced concrete with curved shape

Curved opening toward the sea

Fair-faced concrete with glazing toward the sea

Details of fair-faced concrete

Bench made by poured concrete

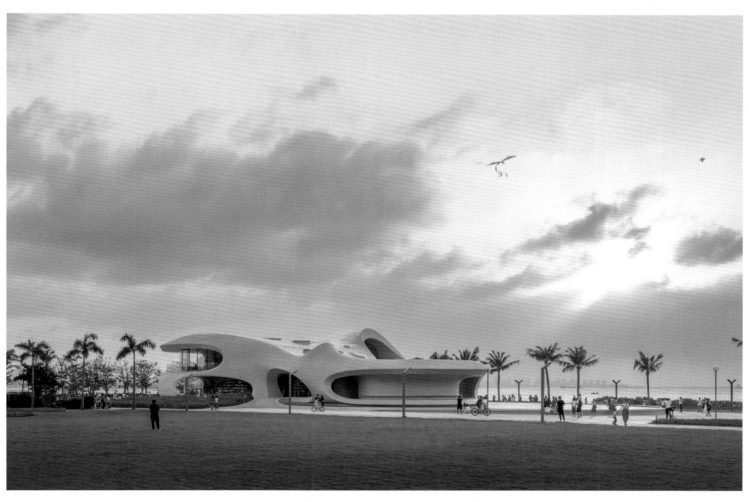

View from the park

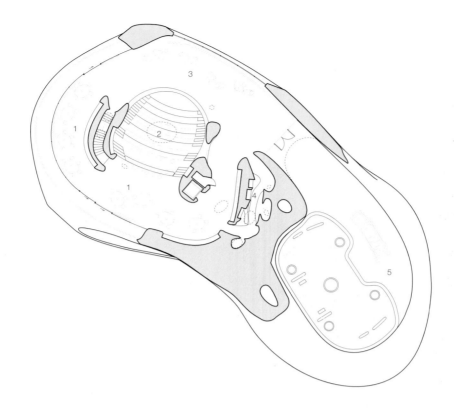

Second-floor plan

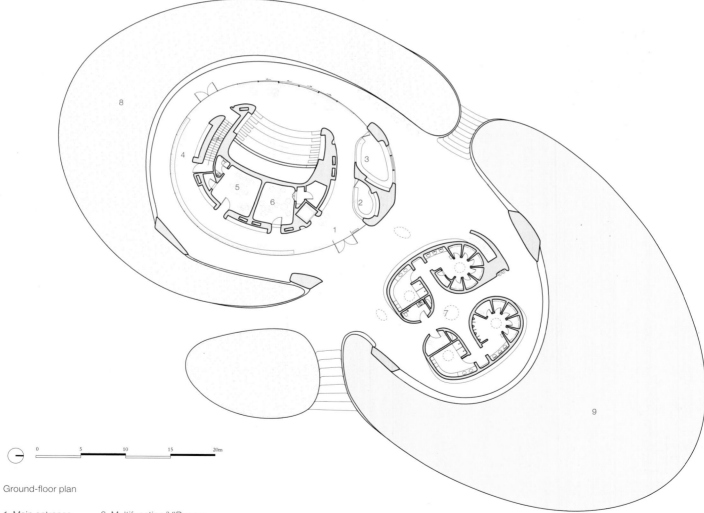

Ground-floor plan

1. Main entrance
2. Reception
3. Café
4. Reading space
5. Office
6. Multifunction/VIP room
7. Bathroom
8. Sand pool
9. Reflecting pool

0   5   10   15   20m

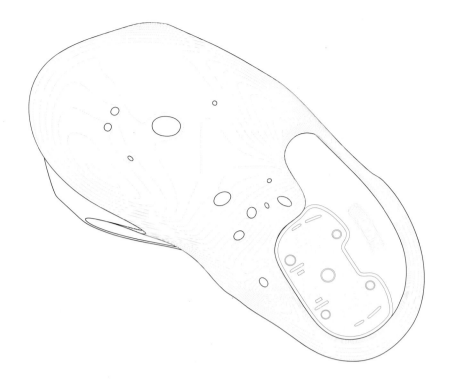

Roof plan

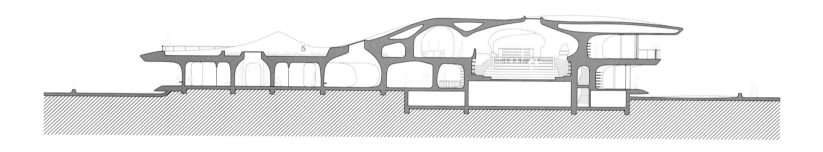

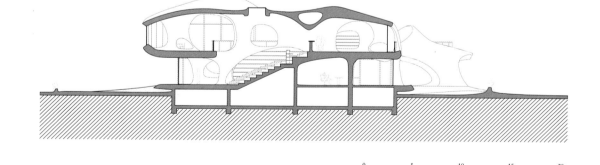

Sections

1. Café
2. Reading space
3. Multifunction/VIP room
4. Bathroom
5. Sand pool
6. Reflecting pool
7. Stepped reading space
8. Ocean view reading space
9. Kids' reading space
10. Roof garden
11. MEP

0   5   10   15   20m

Chapel of Sound

OPEN Architecture

Location: Chengde, Hebei Province, China
Architect: OPEN Architecture
Principal architects: Li Hu, Huang Wenjing
Design team: Zhou Tingting, Fang Kuanyin, Huang Zetian, Lin Bihong, Jia Han, Chen Xiuyuan, Cai Zhuoqun, Kuo Chunchen, Tang Ziqiao
Client: Aranya International Cultural Development Co., Ltd.
Floor area: 790 square meters
Structural & MEP Engineers: Arup
Lighting consultant: Ning Field Lighting Design
Theater & acoustic consultant: JH Theatre Architecture Design Consulting Company
Landscape design: Guangzhou Turen Landscape Planning Co., Ltd.
Design year: 2017–2021
Photography: Jonathan Leijonhufvud, Runzi Zhu, Nan Ni, Right Angle

Site plan

Nestled in a mountainous valley two hours away by car from the center of Beijing, the Chapel of Sound is a monolithic open-air concert hall with views to the ruins of the Ming Dynasty–era Great Wall. Designed by a Beijing-based architecture office, OPEN, to look like a mysterious boulder that had gently fallen into place, the building is built entirely from concrete that is enriched with an aggregate of local mineral-rich rocks, and encompasses a semi-outdoor amphitheater, outdoor stage, viewing platforms, and a green room. While designed to capture the unfamiliar and deeply touching experience of music performed in the cradle of nature, the architects also wanted people just to calm down and listen to the sound of nature, which they believe is profoundly inspiring and healing. When there is no performance, the concert hall is also a tranquil space for contemplation and community gatherings with stunning views of the sky and the surrounding landscape.

OPEN's founding partners, Li Hu and Huang Wenjing, were driven by a desire to minimize the footprint of the concert hall in the valley, creating a structure that was in dialogue with impressive natural landscape, while also feeling undeniably created. The resulting rock-like structure is composed of an inner and outer shell with the space between operating like a truss, and was ultimately achieved through close collaboration with an international engineering firm, Arup. Formed from concrete, each striation cantilevers out from the previous layer to create the inverted cone shape. Winding staircases weave through the building to a rooftop platform that offers panoramic views of the valley and Great Wall. In the interior spaces, accents of bronze for details such as handrails and doors are used to create a warm contrast against the concrete.

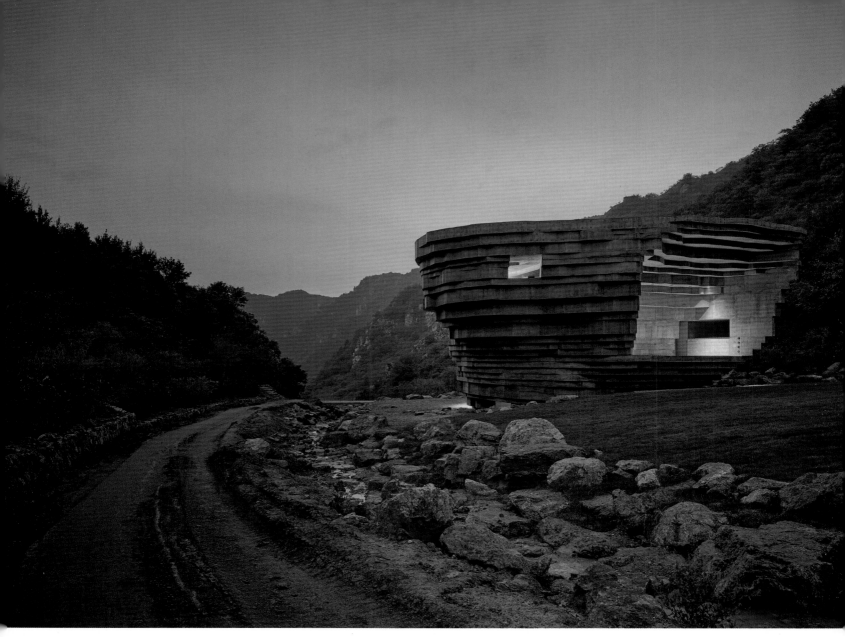

Outdoor stage facing a gentle slope

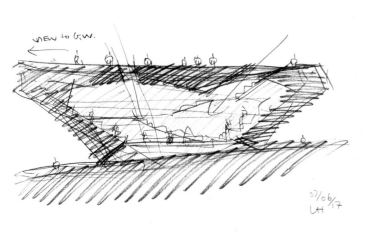

Sketch by Li Hu

Valley covered in snow

Inverted cone-shaped structure

Opening on the roof

The brief for the project was very open, which inspired the architects to research all aspects of performance, looking at how the behaviors of sound could be a driving force behind the final shape of a building; Li and Huang described wanting to: "see the shape of sound." Ultimately, they were drawn to the ways sound reverberates in natural spaces such as caves. Having designed theaters and concert halls, they knew the challenges were how to create excellent acoustic environments without introducing additional sound-absorbing materials. Working with acoustic engineers, OPEN looked at the many ways people experience sound in the concert hall, and defined openings that act both as the sound absorption areas and provide a connection with the exterior environment. OPEN said:

We were very aware of the responsibility we had to contribute a thoughtful structure that fits naturally into such a unique landscape. We wanted to create something different, and more importantly, something meaningful. We are now at a time that the question of our relationship with nature as human beings is more acute than ever. Can we be humble enough to hear what nature is murmuring to us? The symphony of nature is what we really wanted people to experience here.

Openings on the wall

Rooftop viewing terrace

Steel stairs to the roof

Steel stairs detail

There is an inherent air of mystery around the Chapel of Sound that draws you in as you approach the building. This extends to how people will interact with the space: from being a place for individual reflection to a venue for large-scale concerts, the structure can be experienced in many different ways. Huang said: "We wanted the definition of the space to be not so absolute, thus allowing for possibilities. Solitary or communal, music or sound of nature, gazing into the starry sky or connecting with one's inner self—it's open to the interpretation of the users."

Semi-outdoor amphitheater at night

Semi-outdoor amphitheater

Semi-outdoor amphitheater

The double shell structure

Valley view from the terrace

Clockwise from left:
Skylight above the stage;
Signage;
The canyon path

With no heating or air-conditioning, the Chapel of Sound consumes minimal energy, something OPEN was very conscious of when designing the building. The openings also allow the natural elements to come inside, a void in the center of the rooftop allowing daylight to enter the structure and naturally illuminate the performance spaces. When it rains, the water will also cascade through the void; however, inspired by the Pantheon, OPEN designed a drainage system that quickly drains the water away.

Li and Huang spent over ten years training and working in the United States, and as a result are very conscious of moving away from traditionally "Eastern" or "Western" ideas of architecture, particularly when it comes to cultural spaces. OPEN understands that the perceived differences in how cultures experience events and spaces are overstated, and through their architecture, they strive to demonstrate that architecture has the power to connect people with each other, with nature, and with our own past and future.

Second-floor corridor

Ground-floor corridor

Stairway

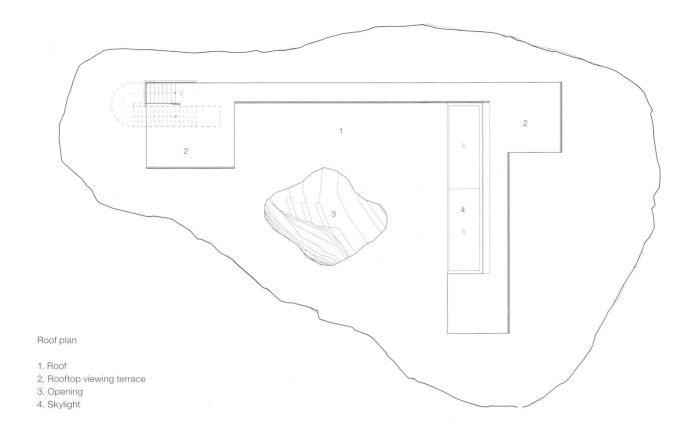

Roof plan

1. Roof
2. Rooftop viewing terrace
3. Opening
4. Skylight

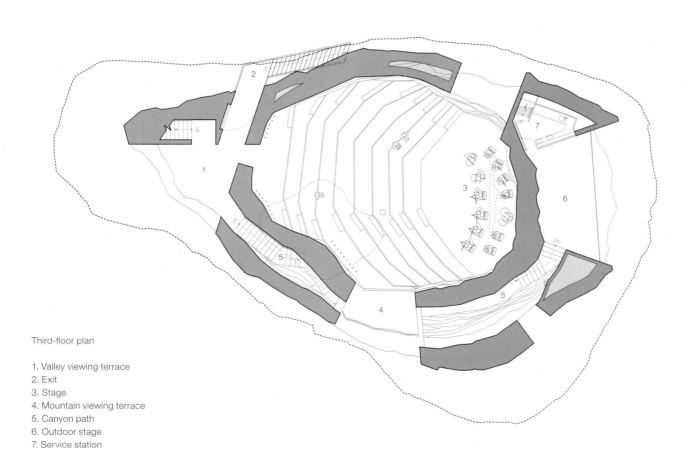

Third-floor plan

1. Valley viewing terrace
2. Exit
3. Stage
4. Mountain viewing terrace
5. Canyon path
6. Outdoor stage
7. Service station

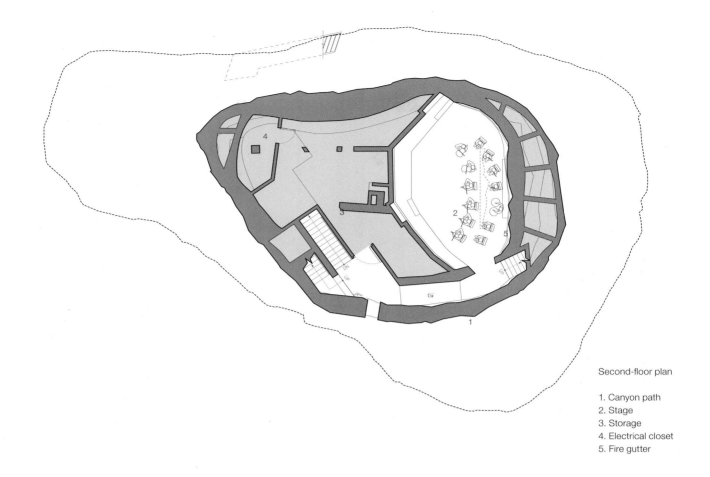

Second-floor plan

1. Canyon path
2. Stage
3. Storage
4. Electrical closet
5. Fire gutter

Ground-floor plan

1. Entry
2. Restroom
3. Dressing room
4. Green room
5. Storage

0   1M   5M   10M

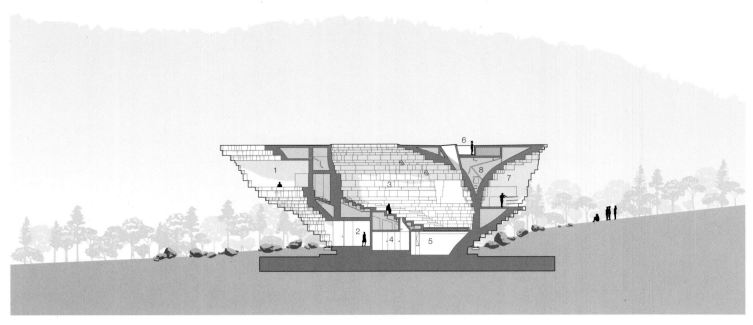

Section A-A

1. Valley viewing terrace
2. Entry
3. Auditorium
4. Corridor
5. Green room
6. Rooftop viewing terrace
7. Outdoor stage
8. Cavity

Section B-B

1. Roof terrace
2. Auditorium
3. Green room
4. Exit

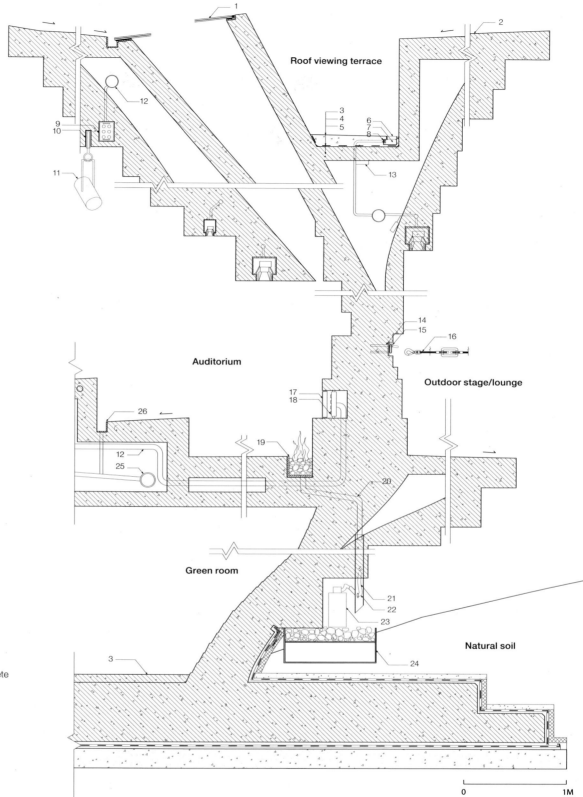

Roof viewing terrace

Auditorium

Outdoor stage/lounge

Green room

Natural soil

0   1M

Detailed drawing of wall

1. Skylight
2. Water repellent concrete
3. Roof concrete floor
4. Waterproofing membrane concrete
5. Structure
6. Stainless-steel grating drainage
7. Gutter
8. LED-lighting strip
9. Integrated lighting control box
10. Stage lighting hanging point
11. Stage lighting
12. Electrical conduit
13. Transformer
14. Embeds
15. Cable hanging bracket
16. Steel cable guardrail steel-cable guardrail
17. Stainless-steel access panel
18. Integrated control box
19. Stainless-steel fire gutter
20. Stainless-steel rainwater drain
21. Gutter
22. Gas pipe casing
23. Temporary gas tank
24. Gravel drainage
25. Rainwater pipe
26. Seating drain

Laurent Troost
Architectures

Project Name: Cassina Innovation House
Location: Manaus, Amazon, Brazil
Design and construction period: 2020
Photography: Joana França

This digital technology center houses spaces to foster creativity and meetings for digital economy makers. The preservation of its ruined condition includes the insertion of an exuberant tropical garden behind the main facade. Those who access the building via the walkway crossing the void over the garden are reminded of the Amazon rainforest. This innovative way of dealing with heritage didn't forget about passive sustainability learnings such as industrial prefabricated steel structure, cross ventilation, permeability, microclimate, large eaves, ventilated void roof, and double-skin frames.

Laurent Troost Architectures

Project Name: Campinarana House
Location: Manaus, Amazon, Brazil
Design and construction period: 2017
Photography: Leonardo Finotti, Maíra Acayaba

In the Amazon, natural conditions require an architecture oriented towards thermal comfort and "passive" sustainability: adequate footprint, protective eaves, dimensioning and orientation of cross ventilation openings, as well as preservation of local ecological systems.

To preserve the pre-existing campinarana—Amazon forest type—the main architectural strategy was to minimize footprint by reversing the classic housing typology: sleeping rooms are located on the ground floor and living spaces on the upper floor.

To optimize exposure to climatic factors, the house was divided into two volumes. The longilineal volume houses functions that do not need to be protected from the sun (access, garage, storage, pool, laundry, quarry) and the transversal one houses functions that need to be protected from the sun (living room, dining room, kitchen, bedrooms).

The transversal volume received a contemporary reinterpretation of the Brazilian colonial roofs, with eight pitches in two levels, allowing the fruition of winds and the creation of an air mattress. On the east and west sides, the roof consists of vertical planes protecting the spaces from the first and last rays of sun. The choice of Corten as roof material was due to its low maintenance and evolutionary character in harmony with the campinarana's reddish clay soil.

Metro Arquitetos +
Paulo Medes da Rocha

Project Name: Cais das Artes (Quay of Arts)
Location: Vitória, Espírito Santo, Brazil
Design and construction period: 2011
Photography: Leonardo Finotti

The Cais das Artes in Vitória is a prominent architectural complex that includes a museum and a theater. It is strategically located on the Suá Bay, offering a comprehensive view of natural and architectural landmarks such as the Vila Velha mountains and the Penha Convent. The complex features an open square accessible to the public, providing a unique perspective of the ocean. The museum has a large exhibition space of 3,000 square meters, while the theater can accommodate up to 1,300 spectators.

Both spaces are complemented by amenities such as cafés, bookstores, and outdoor exhibition areas. The museum's circulation is facilitated by ramps that allow visitors to appreciate the natural surroundings, and the theater includes galleries for easy movement and access to dressing rooms and technical spaces. The Cais das Artes has played a crucial role in the city's urban expansion, attracting significant investments and positioning Vitória as a cultural hub nationally. The design of the complex prioritizes the preservation of the

city's heritage and visually integrates with the landscape.

Overall, the Cais das Artes contributes to the cultural and urban development of Vitória by providing essential infrastructure for major artistic events and enhancing the appreciation of the city's natural and architectural surroundings.

Metro Arquitetos

Project Name: ITA Campus
Location: São José dos Campos, São Paulo, Brazil
Design and construction period: 2017
Photography: Leonardo Finotti

The building designed to house the Fundamental Sciences Department is part of the expansion plan for the ITA campus, which aims to double the number of students in the coming years. It's the first of a number of designed buildings to be built and is part of the Educational Block, which will be completed by the big auditorium, also designed by Metro Architects, and by the new library, designed by MMBB Architects.

The projects for the buildings that are part of this expansion, carried out by a consortium between Metro, Piratininga and MMBB offices, insert themselves in a relevant architectural context—the original project for the campus and the buildings, dating from 1947, are works of Oscar Niemeyer. Through their implantation, they seek to articulate the existing buildings with new constructions in a way that mutually complements and potentializes their uses.

Prefabricated, quickly assembled systems were used, such as metallic structures and precast concrete panels, aiming to reduce deadlines and waste in the building site. These premises made the construction a lot more efficient without, however, reducing the generosity, lightness, and beauty of the buildings, in search of a virtuous relationship with the existing campus.

MMBB Arquitetos +
Ben-Avid + JPG.ARQ

Project Name: Brazilian Pavilion, Expo 2020, Dubai
Location: United Arab Emirates, Dubai
Design and construction period: 2018–2021
Photography: Leonardo Finotti, Joana França

The pavilion features the waters of Brazil—its rivers and mangroves, birthplace of the fertility of life, a natural inheritance that underlies all discourse about sustainability on the planet. With its tensile steel structure and lightweight white fabric, the pavilion is a fabric onto which videos are projected, creating an immersive atmosphere of variable images, sounds, aromas, and temperatures, over an area of undulating, shallow water through which the pavilion's visitors may walk. It is a place of interaction, of an arresting scenic character. It is a stage for the visualization of a nature and culture focused both on preservation and on a future made sustainable through technology.

As in times of flood, when a river overflows its banks, inundating what was once land, the project floods, with a thin layer of water, the whole land of Brazil in Dubai. A uniform, dark topography, made of black pigmented, sanded, non-slip concrete, derives its poetic motif from the Rio Negro in the Amazon basin. On this canvas are depicted beaches and backwaters, creating a grand plaza of water. The structure makes it clear that the ground floor is the primary area for visitors, and that access becomes more restricted the further we move away from it.

Paulo Mendes da Rocha + MMBB Arquitetos

Project Name: SESC 24 de Maio
Location: São Paulo, Brazil
Design and construction period: 2000–2017
Photography: Sérgio Souza, Nelson Kon

We believe that the process of transformation and development of cities such as São Paulo is made by slowly adapting to the changes of customs and way of life of the societies that build them.

The new SESC 24 de Maio—which houses a complex set of recreational and service facilities—occupies the former headquarters of the Mesbla department store in downtown São Paulo, and represents an exemplary challenge of intervening in the context of an urban heritage site.

Taking such context into account the proposed design is set both to contribute effectively to the upgrading of such remarkable area of the city, as well as to readapt the building structure to a completely new set of uses and specific programs. In order to do so, the following basic ideas were outlined: to house a large open square at ground level; to create a new vertical circulation; to structure a variety of open spaces at strategic levels; and to build a generous square on the rooftop.

In order to bring about such goals—which are at the core of the design's challenges and which orient its spatial character—a series of decisions on building techniques and infrastructural supply were adopted, namely: the selective demolition of specific parts of the structure and the construction of a new and autonomous building structure.

SPBR /
Baserga Mozzetti Architett

Project Name: Casa Pico Building
Location: Lugano, Switzerland
Design and construction period: 2013
Photography: Nelson Kon

Thanks to the study completed by Baserga Mozzetti Architetti, this project was already advanced before it even started. SPBR Arquitetos designed an irregular polygon shape structure that would house not only apartments of varying size, but also offices on the ground level, creating a multipurpose building that fell within the height restrictions in Lugano.

Underneath the building is an open passage, with access to either the apartment building or the offices. The office space is placed

slightly sunk into the ground, carefully placed and protected by two structural walls. There are two levels underground comprising the parking garage (with natural ventilation and light) and storage.

The building needed to achieve the Swiss standard for energy consumption, the Minergie, and the designers aimed for a low energy result. Windows are triple glazed, with the south and west facades employing retracting aluminum louvers. Each apartment

has independent mechanically controlled ventilation. The wooden panels outside are ventilated and assembled on a frame that holds successive layers of thermal insulation, vapor barrier, and an inside drywall panel. The final strategy adopted to drastically reduce energy consumption for heating and cooling was the inclusion of the geothermal system, with four geothermal probes that descend 225 meters in vertical loops into the ground.

SPBR /
ANGELO BUCCI

Project Name: Weekend House in São Paulo
Location: São Paulo, Brazil
Design and construction period: 2014
Photography: Nelson Kon

Pool and solarium were displayed as parallel volumes. Two columns were located in the 1-meter-wide gap between them. The 12-meter span is faced on one side by beams supporting the pool and on the other by beams that support the solarium and also hang the floor underneath. Structurally, the mass of the pool counterweights the volume which holds inhabited spaces. In other words, water is balanced by the beach.

The ground level was kept free from any construction in order to achieve the maximum garden area ratio. As a result there are three different layers or three levels for three different moods: ground level (garden—introspective or encompassed by the site limits), apartment level (the only indoor space floating above the ground and underneath the pool), and rooftop (swimming pool and solarium, an extroverted or panoramic space).

This building and its program differs from the focus of traditional architectural projects in two ways: the metropolis becomes a possible place to stay and enjoy during the weekends and elements generally considered secondary in a big house become fundamental components.

Andrade Morettin Architects

Project Name: IMS–Instituto Moreira Salles
Location: São Paulo, Brazil
Design and construction period: 2017
Photography: Nelson Kon

The Moreira Salles Institute (IMS) stands as a prominent cultural institution in Brazil, now fortified by its new headquarters in São Paulo. Beyond addressing the pragmatic need for more space, the facility embodies the institute's values and spirit, serving as both a symbolic and programmatic manifestation. Situated on Paulista Avenue, a dynamic hub of diversity and vitality, IMS engages with the city in a direct, accessible manner while offering a serene internal atmosphere.

Strategically positioned 15-meters above street level, the ground floor redefines the relationship between the museum, the city, and its denizens. This innovative shift liberates the museum from the constraints of its lot, transforming it into a vibrant, open space that connects seamlessly with its urban surroundings. As visitors ascend from the bustling sidewalk to the elevated ground floor, the sensory experience evolves, attenuating street noise and altering light dynamics. The architecture orchestrates a transition from city scale to museum scale, culminating in a panoramic view that signifies a departure from immediate street confrontation.

The new IMS embodies a harmonious blend of energy and tranquility, offering a distinctive and subjective encounter for its patrons. This architectural endeavor not only expands the physical footprint but also elevates the immersive potential, redefining the museum's role within the dynamic tapestry of São Paulo.

Andrade Morettin Architects

Project Name: Jardim Lidiane–Social Housing
Location: São Paulo, Brazil
Design and construction period: 2019
Photography: Vinicius Andrade

Situated adjacent to the Marginal Tietê and bordered by the access ramp of the Júlio de Mesquita Neto Bridge in São Paulo's northern zone, the Lidiane housing complex faces challenges within an industrial area with difficult access and frequent flooding. Currently undergoing transformation, the neighborhood houses both favela communities and a burgeoning middle-class population, yet lacks essential communal services and public spaces.

Recognizing the pivotal role of the vibrant street commerce along Sampaio Correia Street in shaping community dynamics, the project focuses on creating quality communal spaces. The centerpiece is a central square at the heart of the complex, designed to extend its positive impact beyond, improving the entire community and surroundings. This square, equipped with sports facilities and public amenities, serves as a structuring element, guiding the organization of nearby buildings and enhancing leisure options.

Surrounding the square, a loggia incorporates commercial areas, public facilities, a telecenter, a reading point, and a space for the residents' association. Preservation of the existing commercial activity on Sampaio Correia Street is deemed vital for the economic and social resilience of the community. Proposing a new road for vehicular circulation and improved access to public transportation, the project aims to integrate the favela with the surrounding neighborhood.

Emphasizing integration and accessibility, the design retains a significant portion of pre-existing structures, with open stairs and elevated walkways connecting units while maintaining privacy. Covered gathering squares at intersections visually connect the complex with neighboring buildings, reinforcing the inclusive strategy within the formal city surroundings. Ultimately, the project envisions not only architectural enhancements but also an upliftment of the community's social fabric.

Brasil Arquitetura

Project Name: Bread Museum–Colognese Mill
Location: llopolis, Rio Grande do Sul, Brazil
Design and construction period: 2005
Photography: Nelson Kon

Two new units in concrete and glass pose a dialogue with the old wooden mill, in a contemporary—and quite Brazilian—language. A hundred years set them apart, but an idea unites them; and that idea is precisely the celebration of the woodwork. Everything there is araucaria wood: the mill; all its apparatus; the new terrace and walkway that recall the houses of the immigrants; the brise-soleil sliding panels; the capitals on the pillars, reminiscent of the fantastic internal structure of the mills; and even the reinforced concrete.

Over time, all of these elements meshed in their appearance by the grayish tone of the aging wood: Mimesis at a distance and the truth of the materials when seen up close.

In this small ensemble, all is museum and museology, including the architecture, the garden, the objects, and their meaning. The main artifact of the museum is the mill itself. In the yard, a collection of millstones of granite and basalt with several shades and levels of hardness, intended for different types of milling

work, be it corn or wheat; in the surroundings, a small water canal fed by a spring under the mill gives the lot its boundaries.

Brasil Arquitetura

Project Name: Praça das Artes (Performing Arts Centre)
Location: São Paulo, Brazil
Design and construction period: 2006
Photography: Nelson Kon

The new building unfurls in three directions; like an octopus, it extends its tentacles and occupies spaces. The main element to establish dialogue with the remaining buildings of the block and the surrounding area is a set of pigmented, exposed concrete edifications, with a total area of 28,500 square meters, suspended over the urban walkways.

The old Dramatic and Musical Conservatory of São Paulo was incorporated to the complex as a space for recitals and exhibits. Once restored, this edifice was integrated to an ensemble of new buildings which hold the facilities of the schools of music and dance, as well as other installations of the Municipal Theater—the orchestra, the city ballet and choir, the documentation center, restaurants, parking lots, and other communal areas.

Besides supplying the long-lasting demand for a working space for the Municipal Theater, this new cultural complex plays a strategic role in the requalification of the central areas of the city, by giving priority to pedestrians. It establishes the public aspect of its rich and complex use class program, by focusing on professional and educational activities related to music and dance, in order to foster urban life and shared living.